kindergarten
FOUNDATIONS

K

American Education Publishing™
An imprint of Carson-Dellosa Publishing LLC
Greensboro, North Carolina

American Education Publishing™
An imprint of Carson-Dellosa Publishing LLC
P.O. Box 35665
Greensboro, NC 27425 USA

ISBN 978-1-62399-076-3

02-097147784

Table Of Contents

Table Of Contents

Table Of Contents

Table Of Contents

Kindergarten can be a year of transition for your child. It is a year that allows children to:
- adjust to a new routine.
- make new friends.
- learn to be responsible.

However, your child is also learning a lot of new things in a short amount of time. By completing this workbook, your child will not only be mastering these basic skills, but also building confidence and the desire to learn.

Kindergarten Foundations offers activities for a full year of practice. The practice pages are simple and engaging, providing hours of learning fun. Many activities also connect with science or social studies for a wide range of learning. With *Kindergarten Foundations*, your child is getting a well-rounded supplement to his or her education.

Language Arts

As a kindergartner, your child will begin to learn the basics of English grammar when writing and speaking. With *Kindergarten Foundations*, he or she will gain more of an exposure of the English language, and with more exposure will come greater confidence and understanding.

In kindergarten, your child will learn:

- to recognize and print upper- and lowercase letters. **pages 14, 17–48**
- to practice his or her handwriting. **pages 17–42**
- to recognize and use high frequency words. **pages 76–77**
- long and short vowels and the sounds that they make. **pages 78–94**

A strong understanding of language arts will help your child in learning how to read, which is vitally important to his or her education. A love of reading almost always leads to a love of learning. It stimulates your child's imagination and encourages creativity, as well as building language skills. Many teachers say that reading to or with your child is the most important thing you can do. Here are fun ways to expose your child to a love of reading and learning:

- Label objects around your house so that your child will learn to associate the object with the printed word. Index cards written with colored markers work well.

- Help your child to understand that print has meaning by encouraging him or her to "read" cereal boxes and other objects around the house.
- In the car, encourage your child to "read" the signs, such as "Stop," "Yield," "Railroad Crossing," etc. Explain what these signs mean and why they are important.
- Use magazines, newspapers, and coloring books to create letter and word collages.
- Celebrate a "letter of the day" (or week) in your home!

Math

As a kindergartner, your child will be learning the basics of math. With *Kindergarten Foundations*, your child will gain the ability to make sense of math problems and persevere in solving them. These skills are the building blocks for your child's success throughout all their years of schooling.

In kindergarten, your child will learn:

- number word recognition. **pages 106–107, 117**
- to identify and describe shapes. **pages 118–121**
- more and less. **pages 127–131**
- addition and subtraction. **pages 143–160**
- basics of measurement. **pages 167–170**
- telling time. **pages 171–175**

Your child will become more interested in math if he or she can see how it applies to life outside of school. Here are fun ways to practice age-appropriate math with your child throughout each day:

- Have your child trace your hand. Have your child trace his or her hand and compare their sizes. Whose hand is longer? Whose hand is shorter?
- Use paper clips as a unit of measurement and measure objects around your house.
- Ask your child: How old are you? How many candles were on your birthday cake? How many candles will be on your cake next year?
- Make a chart with your child that lists his or her daily routine. For example: 8:00 — time to wake up!
- Create kitchen pattern art with your child. Use cereal, macaroni, or other small foods to create patterns. Glue the finished design to colored construction paper.

Language Arts

Long e

Sunflower Circles

Directions: Trace each circle. Start at the dot.

Try This!

Use craft materials to decorate the sunflower above.

10

All Sorts of Things

Directions: Cut out each object. Sort each into the correct category. Color the pictures.

What Doesn't Belong?

Directions: Draw an **X** on the picture in each row that does not belong.

   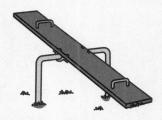

3 10 B 4

Tell why each picture does not belong in the activity above.

Fancy Feathers

Directions: Color the letters blue. Color the numbers green.

Count the letters in the peacock above.
How many letters are there in all?

14

House of Letters

Directions: Cut. Sort. Glue.

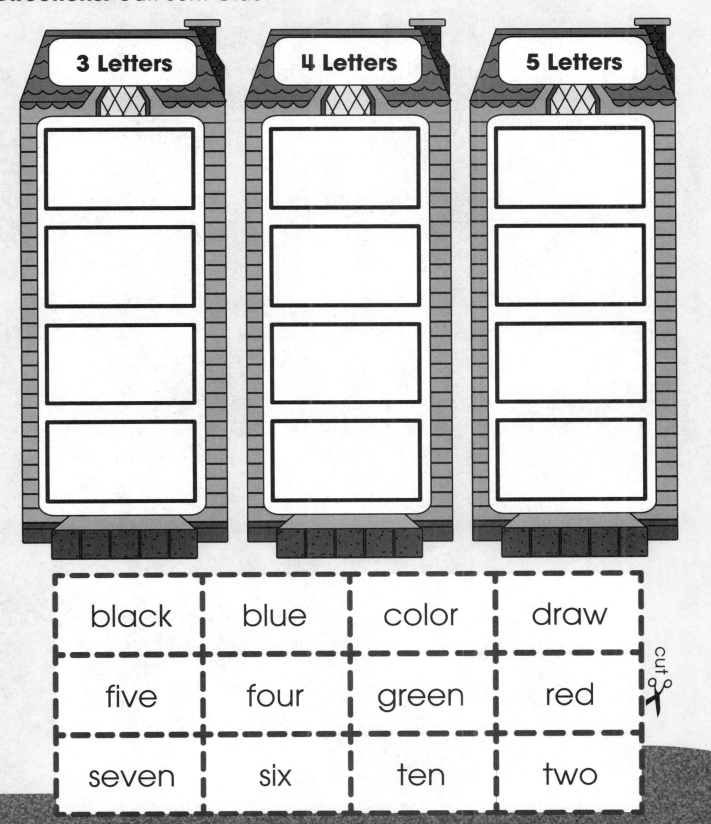

3 Letters

4 Letters

5 Letters

black	blue	color	draw
five	four	green	red
seven	six	ten	two

cut

15

Know Your Letters: Aa

Directions: Trace each letter. Write five on your own. Circle your best letter.

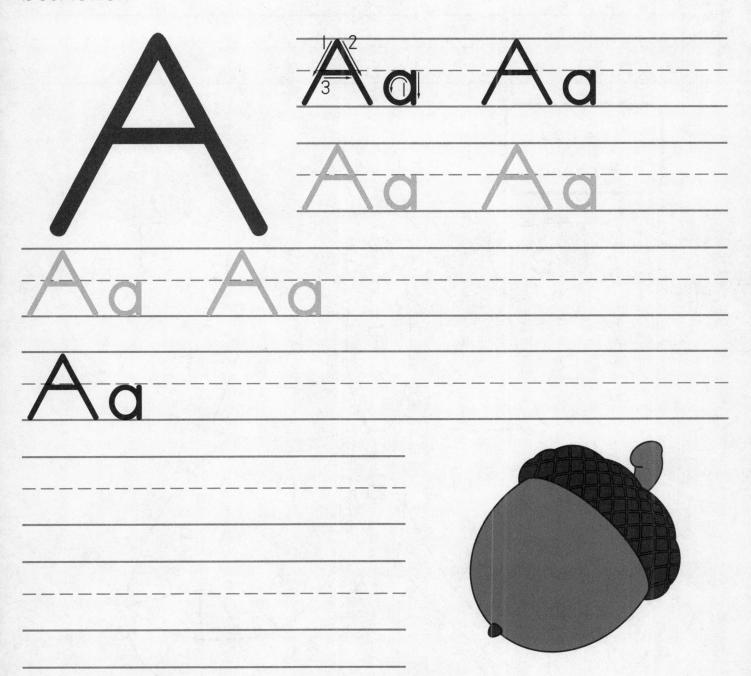

Tear tiny pieces of colored construction paper.
Glue the pieces to the big letter **A** above.

Know Your Letters: Bb

Directions: Trace each letter. Write three on your own. Color the picture.

Bb

B = red
b = orange

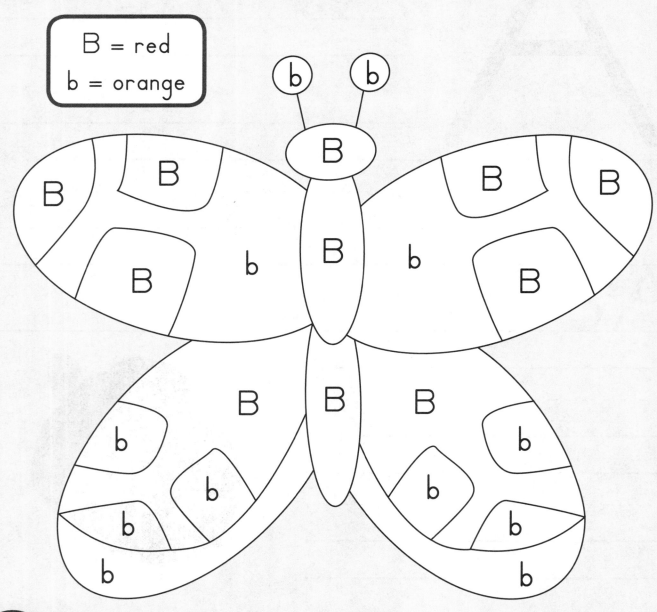

On another sheet of paper, draw three things that start with the letter **B**.

Know Your Letters: Cc

Directions: Trace each letter. Write five on your own. Circle your best letter.

C   Cc   Cc

Cc   Cc

Cc   Cc

Cc

Trace the big letter **C** above with five different colors of crayon.

Know Your Letters: Dd

Directions: Trace each letter. Write three on your own. Color the picture.

Dd

| D = black | d = brown |

 **Try This!**

On another sheet of paper, draw something a dog might like to do.

Know Your Letters: Ee

Directions: Trace each letter. Write five on your own. Circle your best letter.

E

E e E e

E e E e

E e E e

E e

Try This!

Twist tiny pieces of colorful tissue paper. Glue the pieces to the big letter **E** above.

Know Your Letters: Ff

Directions: Trace each letter. Write three on your own. Color the picture.

Ff

| F = purple | f = red |

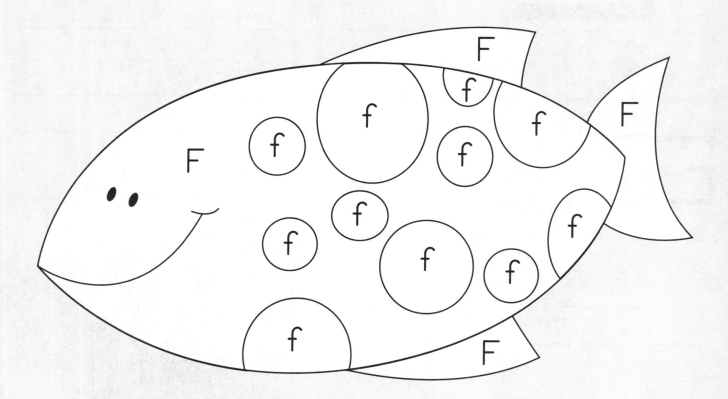

Know Your Letters: Gg

Directions: Trace each letter. Write five on your own. Circle your best letter.

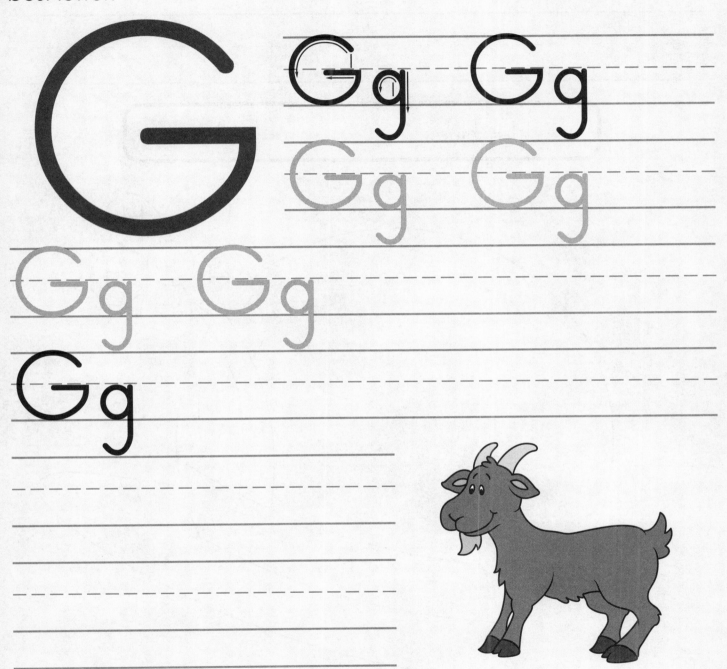

Cut small pieces of yarn.
Glue the yarn to the big letter **G** above.

Directions: Trace each letter. Write three on your own. Color the picture.

Hh

H = blue   h = yellow

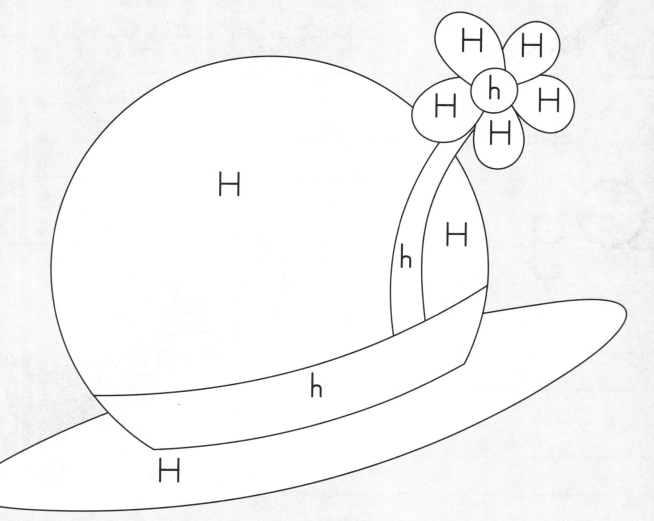

On another sheet of paper, write three words that begin with the letter **H**.

Know Your Letters: Ii

Directions: Trace each letter. Write five on your own. Circle your best letter.

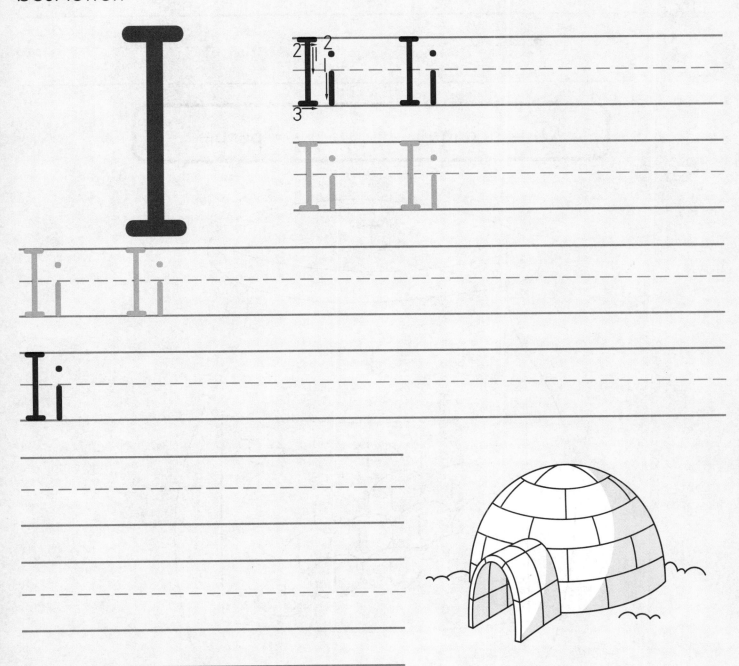

Glue craft supplies to decorate the big letter **I** above.
Use glitter, beads, sequins, wooden craft sticks, or anything else you have.

25

Directions: Trace each letter. Write three on your own. Color the picture.

Jj

J = orange   j = purple

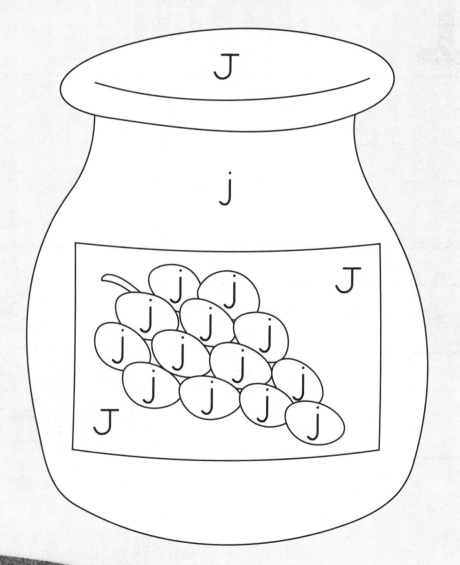

Try This!

On another sheet of paper, write a list of things you could place in a jar. Try to write words that begin with the letter **J**.

Know Your Letters: Kk

Directions: Trace each letter. Write five on your own. Circle your best letter.

K   Kk   Kk

Kk   Kk

Kk   Kk

Kk

Twist tiny pieces of colorful tissue paper. Glue the pieces to the big letter **K** above.

Directions: Trace each letter. Write three on your own. Color the picture.

L = yellow   l = brown

On another sheet of paper, write a list of three animals that begin with the letter **L**.

Try This!

28

Know Your Letters: Mm

Directions: Trace each letter. Write five on your own. Circle your best letter.

M

Mm Mm

Mm Mm

Mm Mm

Mm

Cut small pieces of yarn.
Glue the yarn to the big letter M above.

29

Know Your Letters: Nn

Directions: Trace each letter. Write three on your own. Color the picture.

N = brown   n = blue

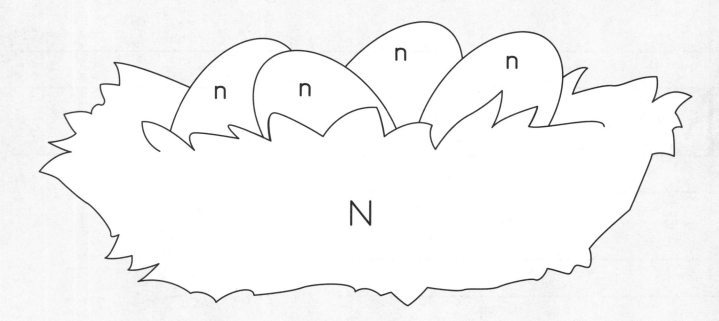

Draw the animal that made the nest in the picture.
Give your animal a name that begins with the letter N.

Know Your Letters: Oo

Directions: Trace each letter. Write five on your own. Circle your best letter.

Twist tiny pieces of colorful tissue paper.
Glue the pieces to the big letter **O** above.

Know Your Letters: Pp

Directions: Trace each letter. Write three on your own. Color the picture.

P p

P = black   p = orange

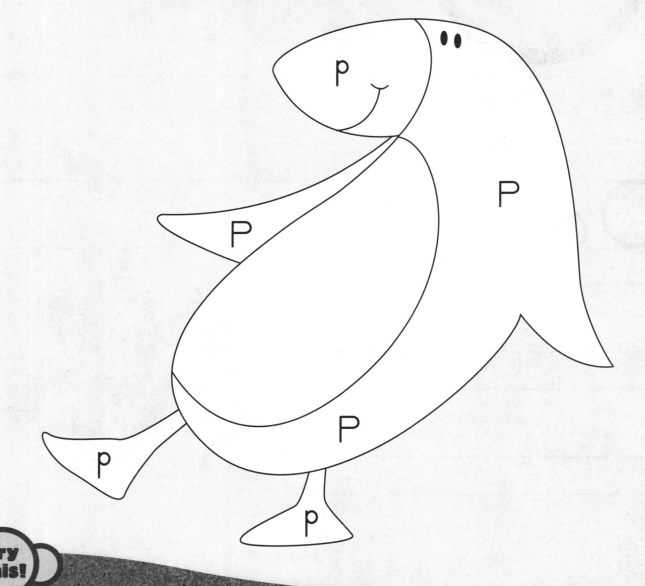

Try This!

On another sheet of paper, write a sentence about penguins.
Use as many words as you can.

32

Know Your Letters: Qq

Directions: Trace each letter. Write five on your own. Circle your best letter.

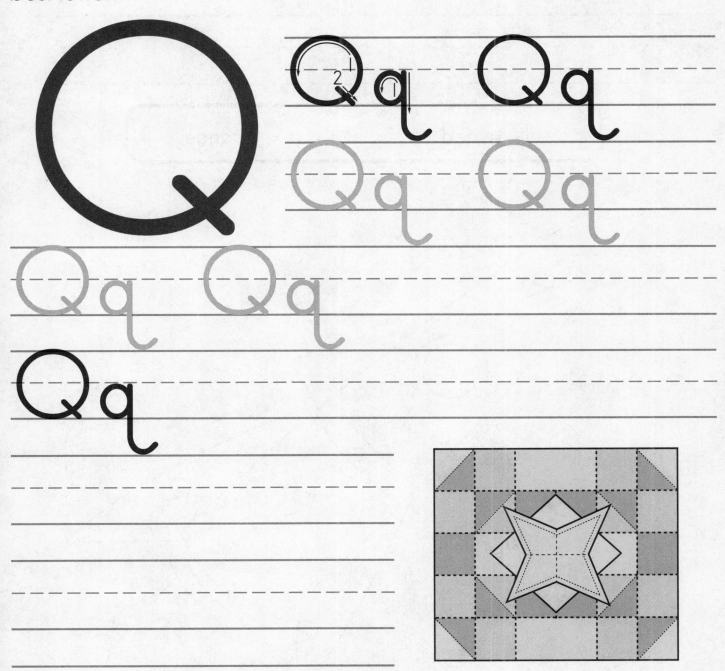

Trace the big letter **Q** above with five different colors of crayon.

Directions: Trace each letter. Write three on your own. Color the picture.

Rr

R = red   r = orange

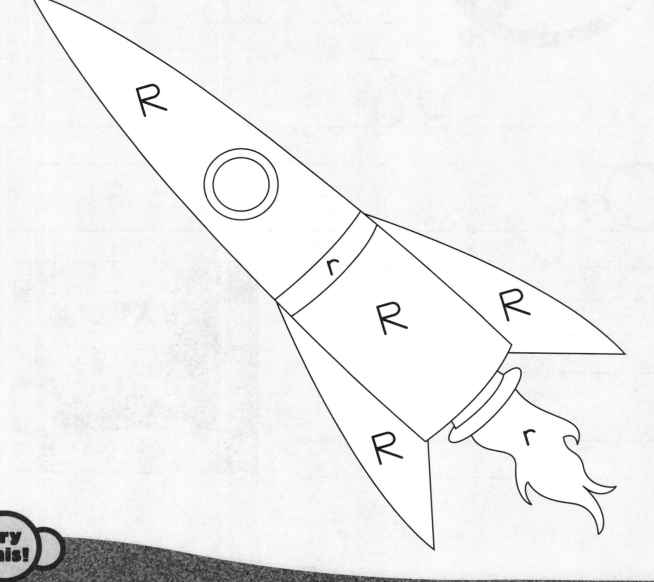

Try This!

On another sheet of paper, use a red crayon to write as many words that begin with the letter **R** as you can.

Know Your Letters: Ss

Directions: Trace each letter. Write five on your own. Circle your best letter.

S Ss Ss

Ss Ss

Ss Ss

Ss

Glue craft supplies to decorate the big letter S above.
Use glitter, beads, sequins, wooden craft sticks, or anything else you have.

Directions: Trace each letter. Write three on your own. Color the picture.

T = pink   t = purple

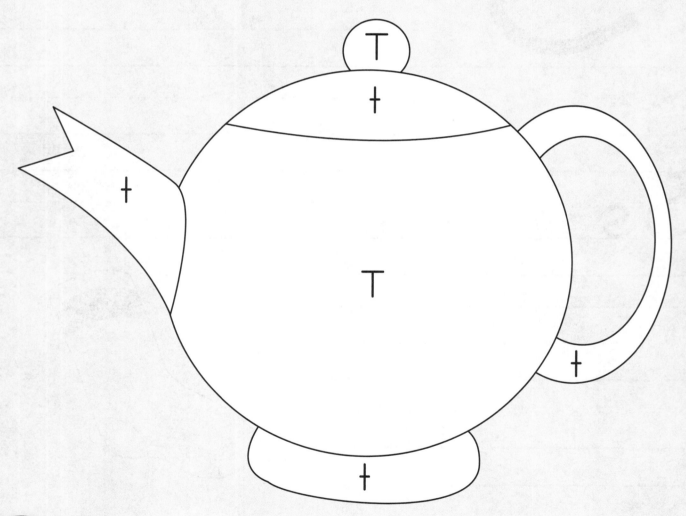

Try This!

Circle every letter **T** that you see on this paper.

Know Your Letters: Uu

Directions: Trace each letter. Write five on your own. Circle your best letter.

Cut small pieces of yarn.
Glue the yarn to the big **letter U** above.

Directions: Trace each letter. Write three on your own. Color the picture.

| V = red | v = gray |

 **Try This!**

Use a violet crayon to write the name of the vulture in the picture.
Give the vulture a name that begins with the letter **V**.

38

Know Your Letters: Ww

Directions: Trace each letter. Write five on your own. Circle your best letter.

Tear tiny pieces of construction paper.
Glue the pieces to the big letter **W** above.

Know Your Letters: Xx

Directions: Trace each letter. Write three on your own. Color the picture.

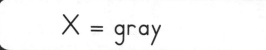

X = gray   x = black

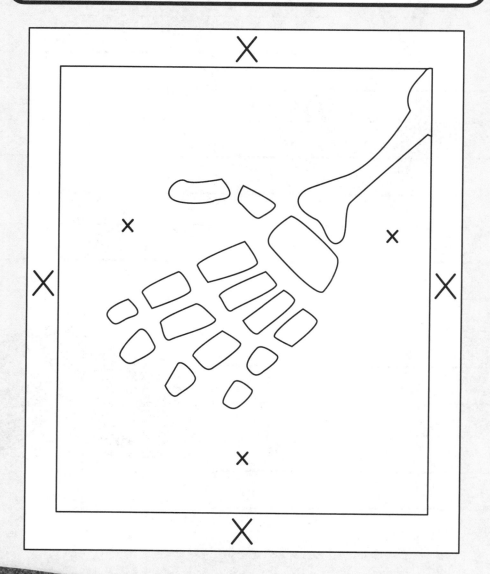

On another sheet of paper, draw a big letter **X**.
Glue pieces of colored construction paper on the letter.

Know Your Letters: Yy

Directions: Trace each letter. Write five on your own. Circle your best letter.

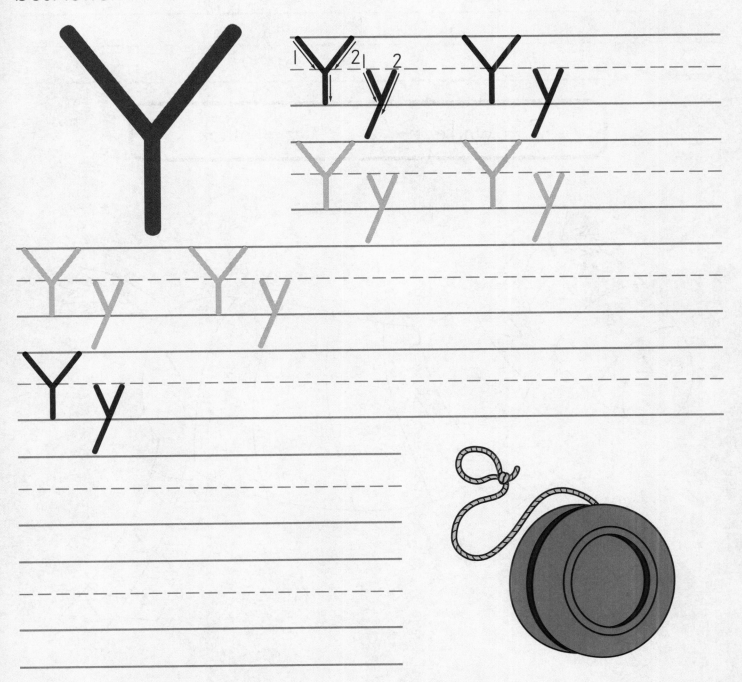

Cut small pieces of yarn.
Glue the yarn to the big letter **Y** above.

Try This!

Directions: Trace each letter. Write three on your own. Color the picture.

Zz

| Z = white | z = black |

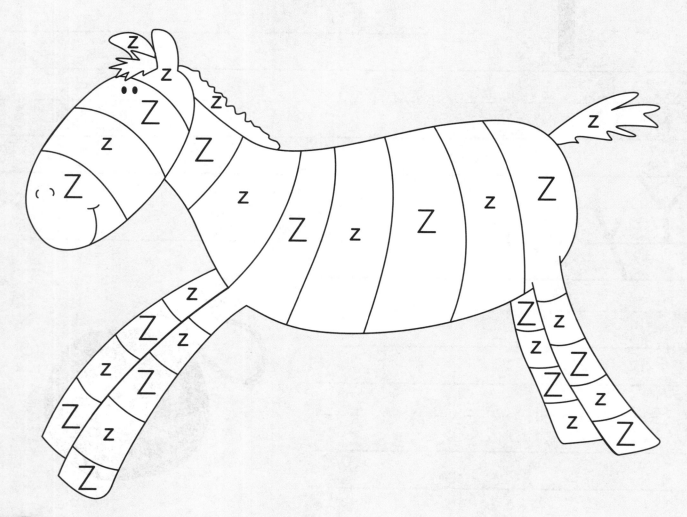

On another sheet of paper, draw three things that start with the letter **Z**.

Treat, Treat!

Directions: Cut out each letter. Glue the letters under the correct dog or puppy. How many uppercase letters do you count? How many lowercase letters do you count?

G

n

k   e   h   R   g

Q   Y   t   i

cut

Flower Power

Directions: Color each uppercase and lowercase letter pair the same color. Hint: You will use 11 different colors.

Circle each uppercase letter in the activity above.

Try This!

Juggling Act

Directions: Color the letter pairs.

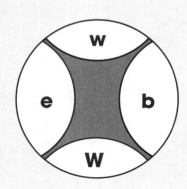
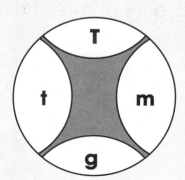
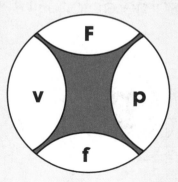

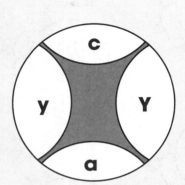
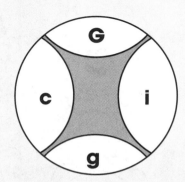
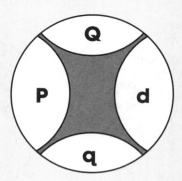

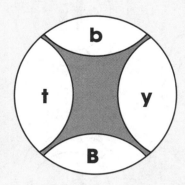
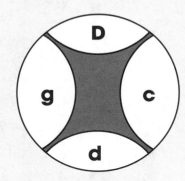
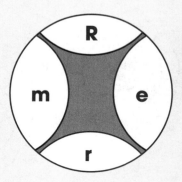

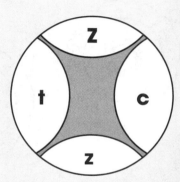

Count the lowercase letters in the activity above.
How many lowercase letters are there in all?

Falling Letters

Directions: Write each lowercase letter on the line.

Try This!

Write the lowercase letters in **ABC** order.

Round and Round

Directions: Write each lowercase letter on the line.

Bear Tracks

Directions: Cut. Glue the tracks in order. Color.

Animal Watch

Directions: Color the path from **A** to **Z**.

Bouncing Beginnings

Directions: Color by the code. Say the name of each picture. Listen to the beginning sound.

b = orange	c = blue	d = yellow	f = red

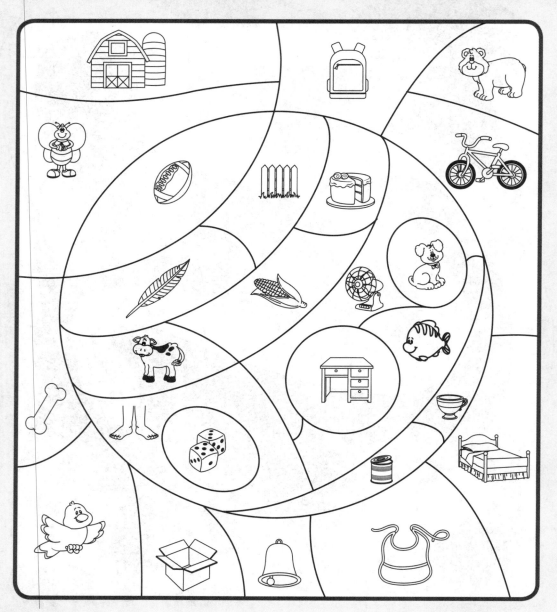

Choose one picture from the activity above.
Write the word for that picture.

Super Sounds

Directions: Color each picture that has the same beginning sound as the first picture. Cut and glue the letters that make the beginning sounds.

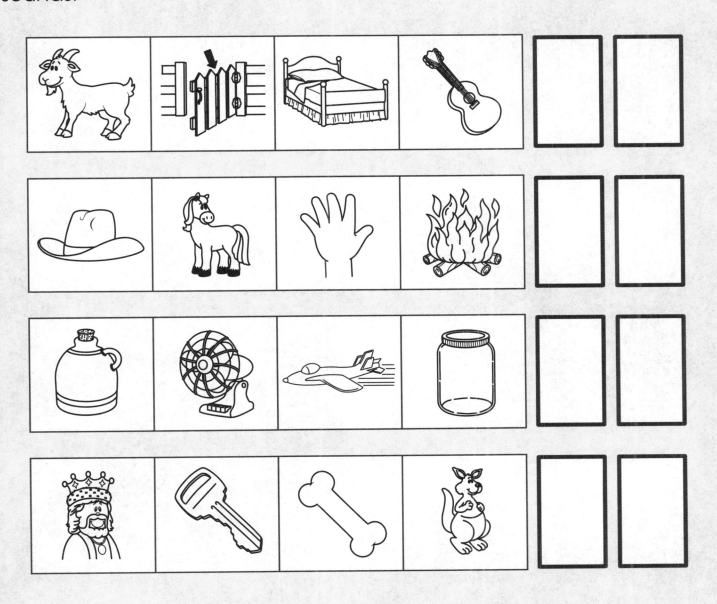

h K H J G j g k

cut

53

Little Words, Big Beginnings

Directions: Write the missing beginning sound. Trace the word.

_eb   _ed   _eg

_et   _og   _est

_ent   _et   _ot

Try This!

Circle the pictures in the activity above that rhyme.

55

Beautiful Beginnings

Directions: Color by the code. Say the name of each picture. Listen to the beginning sound.

l = yellow   m = purple   n = brown   p = blue

Write one word for each letter in the code above.
Draw the pictures in the activity. Color them.

Kite Sounds

Directions: Cut out each picture. Glue it to the kite with the beginning letter.

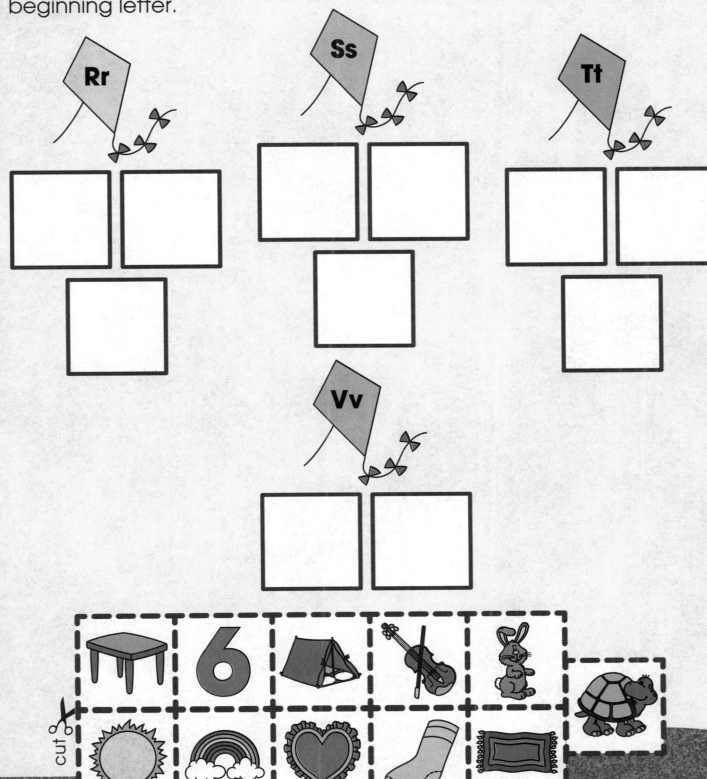

In the End

Directions: Write the missing ending sound. Trace the word.

to**p**

bar**n**

ne**t**

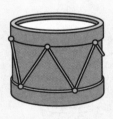
dru**m**

saw

goa**t**

ca**r**

roo**f**

boo**k**

Try This!

Choose three words from the activity above.
Write the words in **ABC** order.

Hot Air Endings

Directions: Say the name of each picture. Listen to the ending sound. Color by the code.

| n = blue | d = orange | p = green |

Try This!

Draw a picture of one more word for each ending letter in the activity above.
Color your drawings by the code above.

60

Race to the Finish

Directions: Say the name of each picture. Listen to the ending sound. Cut out the ending sound. Glue the ending sound to finish the word. Color.

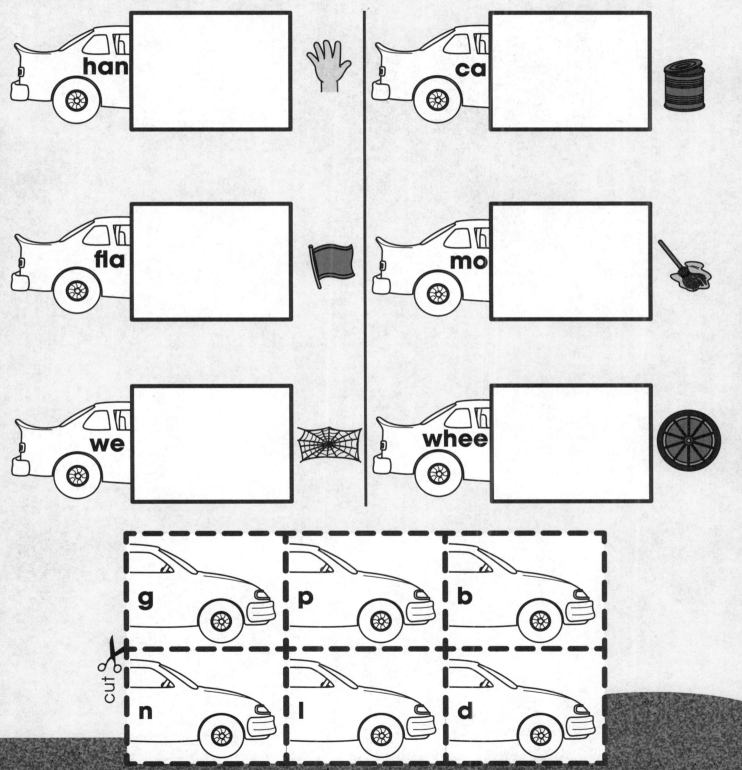

han

ca

fla

mo

we

whee

| g | p | b |
| n | l | d |

cut

Batting Blends

Directions: Cut out each picture. Glue each picture beside the bat with the same beginning blend.

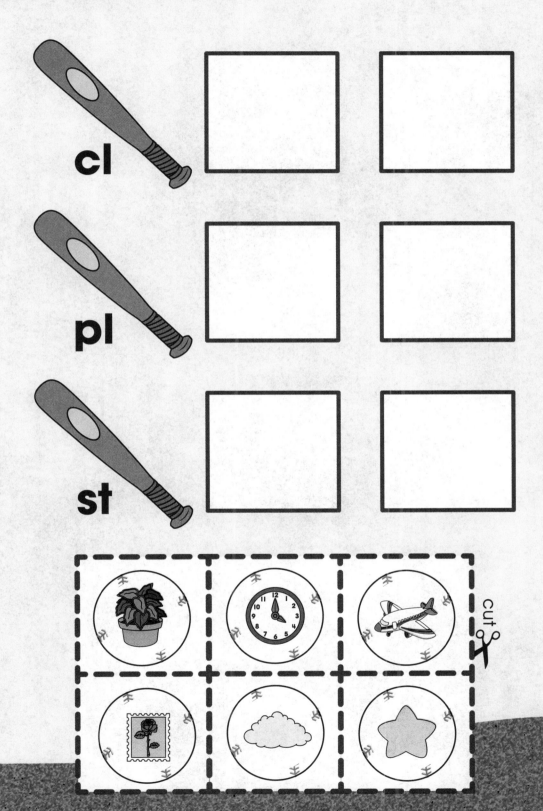

Digging Up Blends

Directions: Cut out each picture. Glue each picture beside the dog with the same beginning sound.

cut

Caps and Shirts

Directions: Cut out each T-shirt. Glue each T-shirt to the cap with the correct beginning blend.

Brilliant Birds

Directions: Say each word. Color by the code.

| th = yellow | sh = blue | ch = red | wh = green |

Try This!

Seashell Syllables

Directions: Color one seashell for each syllable you hear.

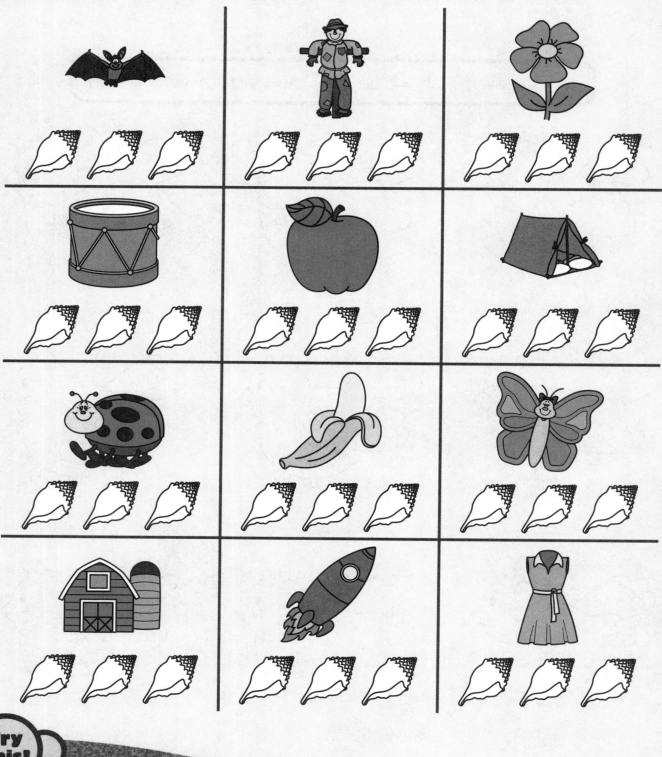

Try This!

Draw a picture of a beach. Include a one-syllable, a two-syllable, and a three-syllable word in your picture.

Counting Syllables

Directions: Say the name of each picture. Count the syllables in each word. Color by the code.

1 = blue	2 = yellow	3 = orange

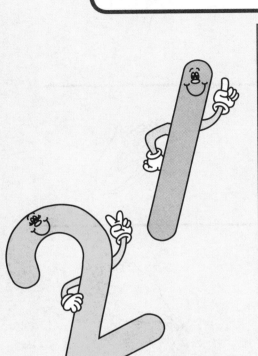

How many words do you count?

_____ 1 syllable   _____ 2 syllables   _____ 3 syllables

Rhyming Buddies

Directions: Circle the word that rhymes with the first word in each row. Color the rhyming pairs.

lamp

horn

nest

hill

net

Fun in the Sun

Directions: Color the rhyming pictures.

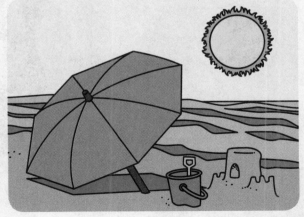

Draw your own set of three words. Two of the words should rhyme and one should not.
Ask a friend to circle the rhyming words.

Try This!

Balloon Colors

Directions: Color the balloons to match their color words.

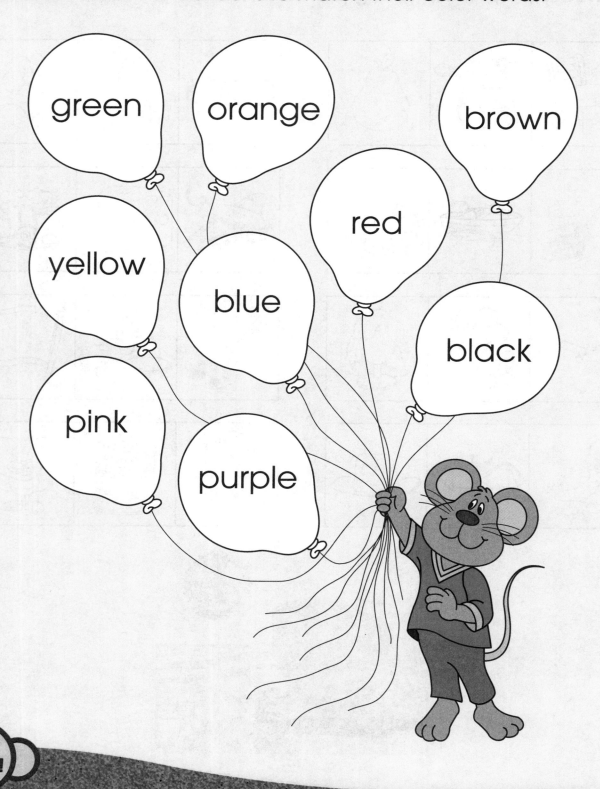

green

orange

brown

red

yellow

blue

black

pink

purple

On another sheet of paper, write each color word in that color of crayon.
For example, write the word **blue** with a blue crayon.

Yum-Yum Gum

Directions: Color each gum ball the correct color. Color the rest of the picture.

Fill in the rest of the gum ball machine with your favorite color gum balls.

Try This!

Sail Away

Directions: Read the words. Use the code to color the picture.

we = yellow	go = orange	see = red
the = purple	and = blue	my = brown

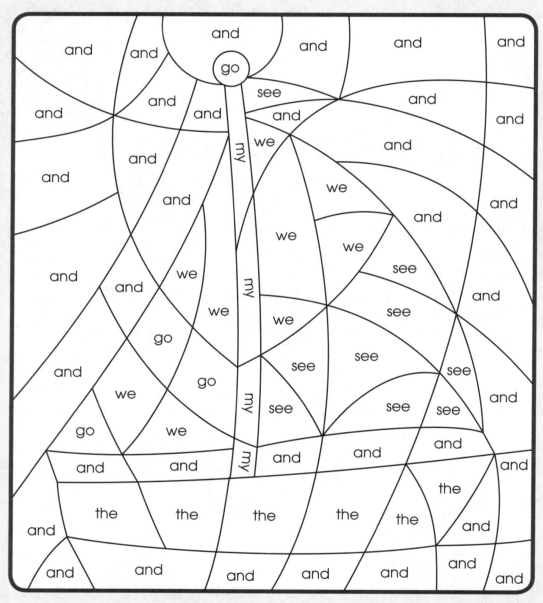

Try This!

Count the number of times each word appears.
Write tally marks next to each word in the code to show the total.

Look for Me

Directions: Color by the code.

she = yellow
is = brown
he = blue
it = green

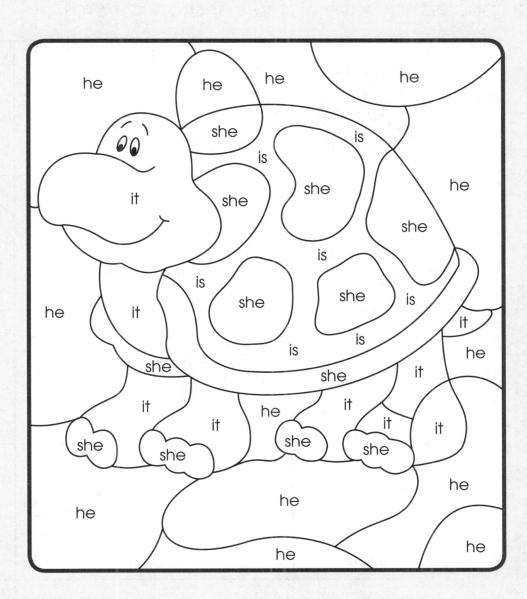

Directions: Trace each word.

is   it   he   she

Say a sentence using each of the high frequency words above.

77

Help the Ant

Directions: Make a path for the ant to get to the anthill. Color the spaces that have pictures of **short a** words.

Choose three pictures that you did not color.
Write the word for each picture.

Find the Nest

Directions: Help the hen find her nest. Make a path for her. Color the pictures that have **short e** in their names.

Start

Finish

Try This!

Choose three pictures that you colored on the path.
Write the words in **ABC** order.

79

Fishing for Short i

Directions: Color each fish that contains a picture of something with **short i** in its name.

Try This!

How many fish did you color in all?

Ollie's Words

Directions: Draw a line from Ollie's arms to the things that have **short o** in their names.

Try This!

On another sheet of paper, write the words for the pictures of **short o** words.

81

Colorful Umbrellas

Directions: Color all of the umbrellas that have pictures of things with **short u** in their names.

Try This!

Cut out an umbrella shape from colored construction paper.
Write as many **short u** words as you can on the umbrella.

Bake a Cake

Directions: Say the name of each picture. Cut. Glue to match with the **short a** or **long a** sound.

Leafy Letters

Directions: Say the name of each picture. Cut. Glue to match with the **short e** or **long e** sound.

Short e

Long e

cut

I Like It!

Directions: Say the name of each picture. Cut. Glue to match with the **short i** or **long i** sound.

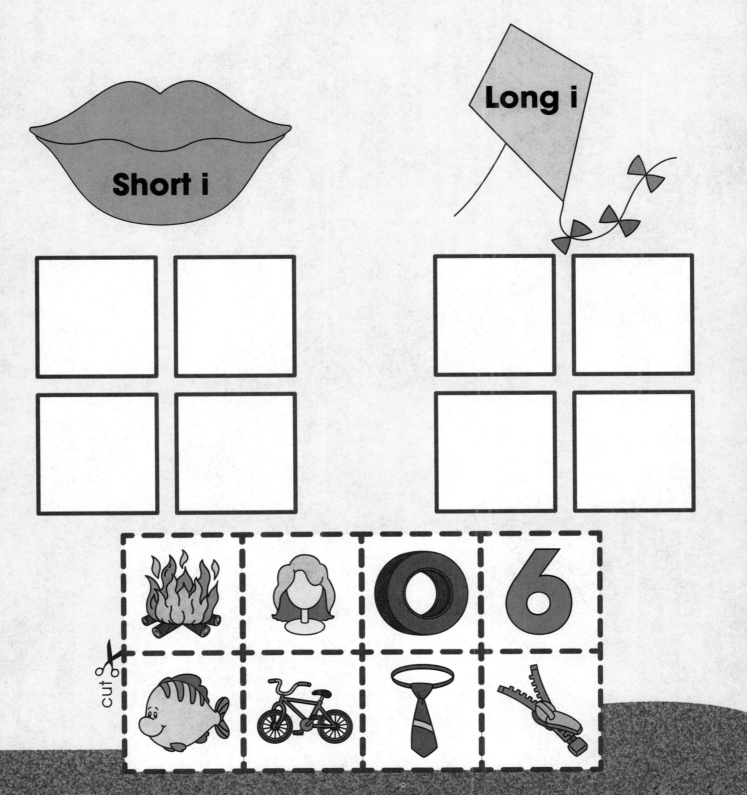

Socks on Top

Directions: Say the name of each picture. Cut. Glue to match with the **short o** or **long o** sound.

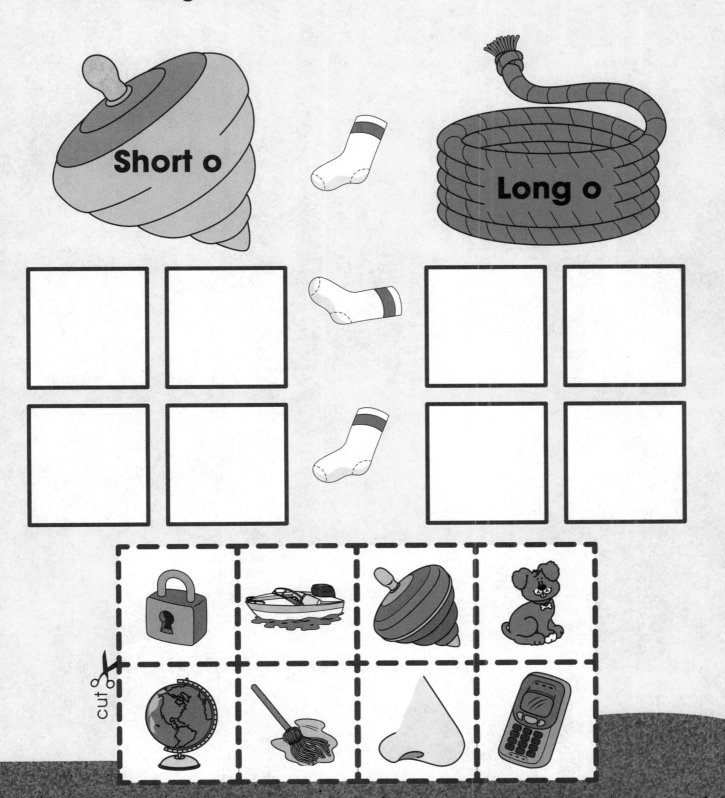

Short o

Long o

cut

Fruity Vowels

Directions: Say the name of each picture. Cut. Glue to match with the **short u** or **long u** sound.

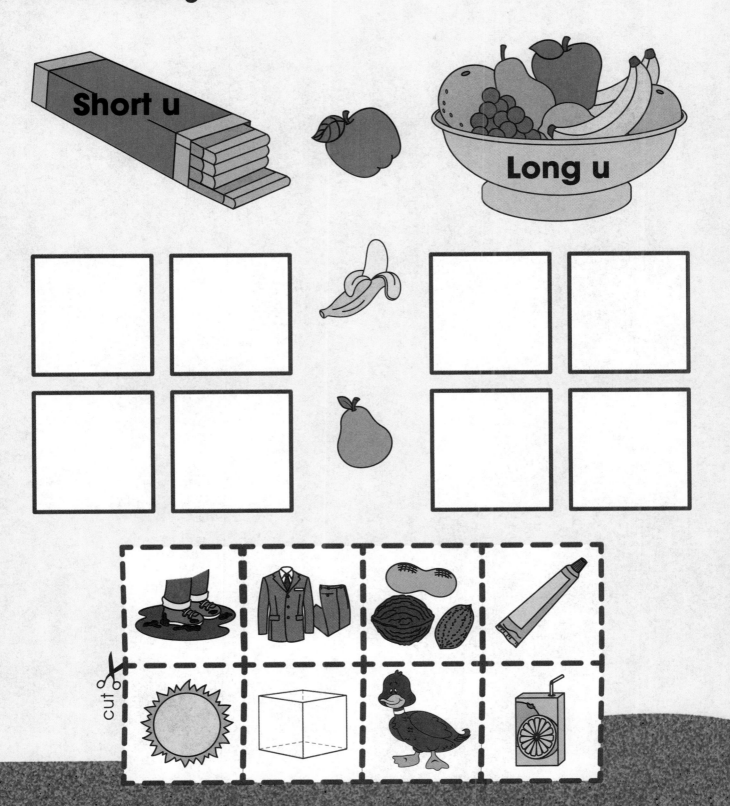

cut

91

Which Vowel?

Directions: Write the missing short vowel: **a**, **e**, **i**, **o**, or **u**.

1. w _____ g

2. 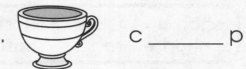 c _____ p

3.  n _____ st

4.  b _____ t

5.  l _____ g

6.  d _____ ck

7. p _____ n

8.  sh _____ ll

9.  h _____ t

10. 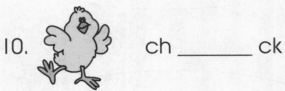 ch _____ ck

11. f _____ n

12. r _____ g

13. m _____ p

14. fr _____ g

15. b _____ d

16. l _____ ck

Try This!

Circle the words that rhyme with matching colors.

Surfer Sounds

Directions: Say the name of each picture. Color by the code.

> **short u** = purple   **short i** = yellow   **short a** = blue
> **short e** = red   **short o** = green

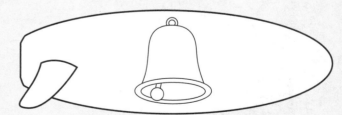

Try This!

Count the number of times each color appears. Write tally marks beside each color in the code to show how many.

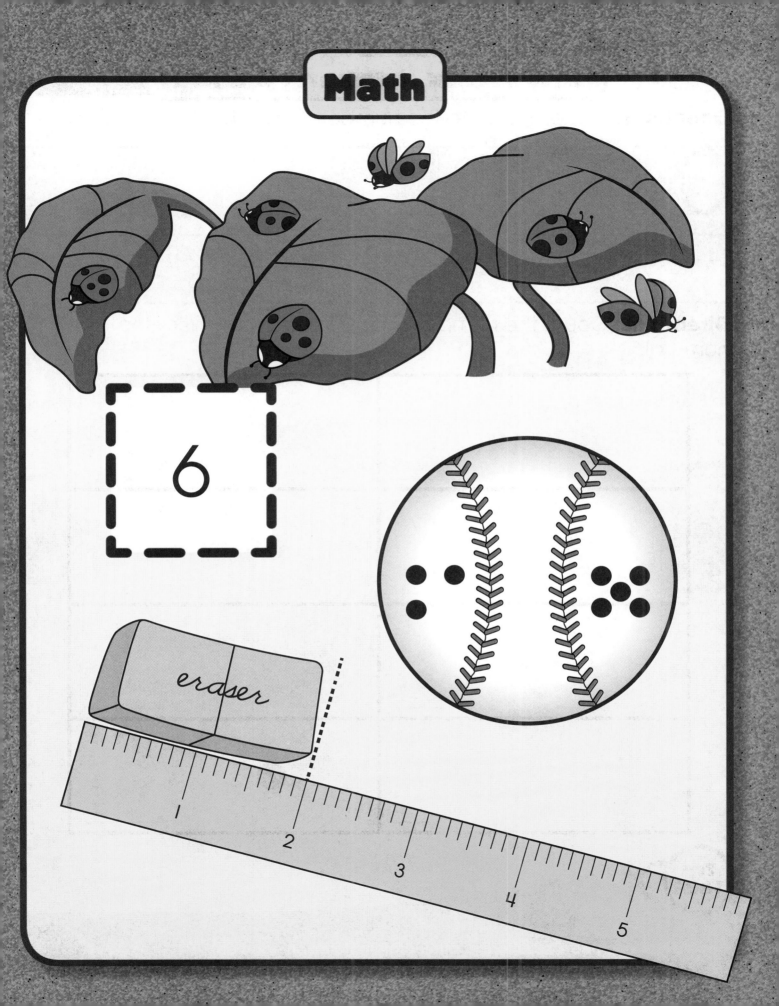

Know Your Numbers: 0 and 1

Directions: Trace and write the numbers 0 and 1.

Directions: Count the number of dots in each set. Write the numeral.

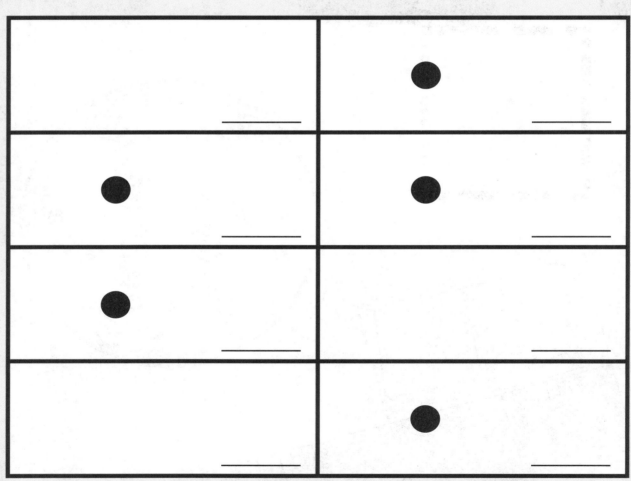

Place a drop of glue on each dot.
Place a bead, a bean, a button, or other craft material on each dot.

Know Your Numbers: 2 and 3

Directions: Trace and write the numbers 2 and 3.

2 2 2 3 3 3

Directions: Count the number of dots in each set. Write the numeral.

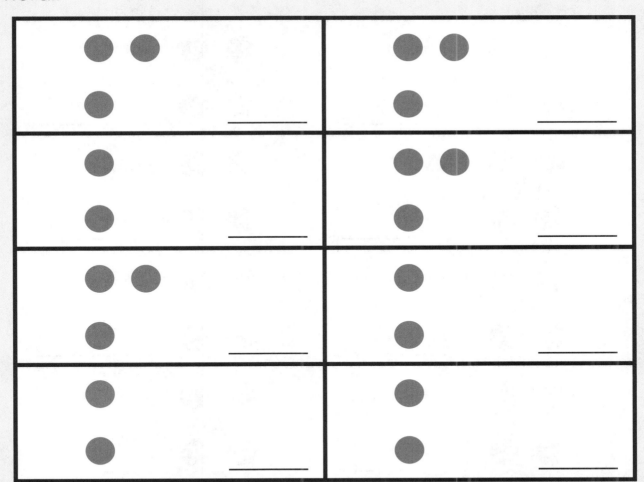

Know Your Numbers: 4 and 5

Directions: Trace and write the numbers 4 and 5.

Directions: Count the number of dots in each set. Write the numeral.

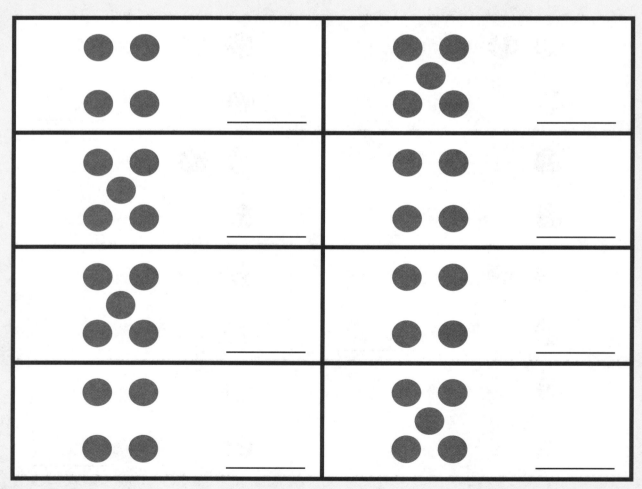

Try This!

Place a drop of glue on each dot.
Place a bead, a bean, a button, or other craft material on each dot.

Know Your Numbers: 6 and 7

Directions: Trace and write the numbers 6 and 7.

Directions: Count the number of dots in each set. Write the numeral.

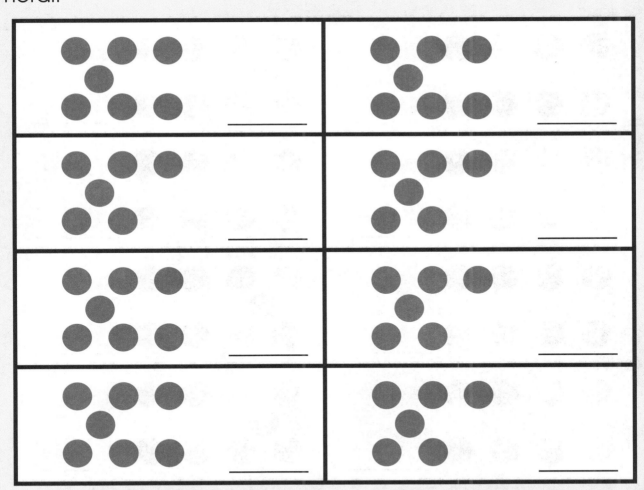

Know Your Numbers: 8 and 9

Directions: Trace and write the numbers 8 and 9.

Directions: Count the number of dots in each set. Write the numeral.

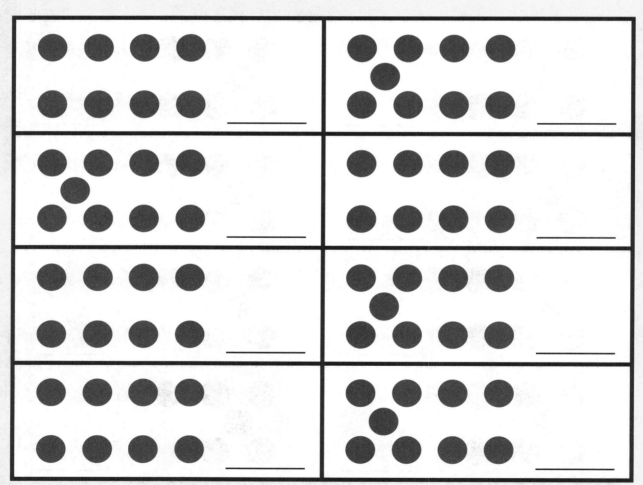

Place a drop of glue on each dot.
Place a bead, a bean, a button, or other craft material on each dot.

Know Your Numbers: 10

Directions: Trace and write the number 10.

Directions: Count the number of dots in each set. Write the numeral.

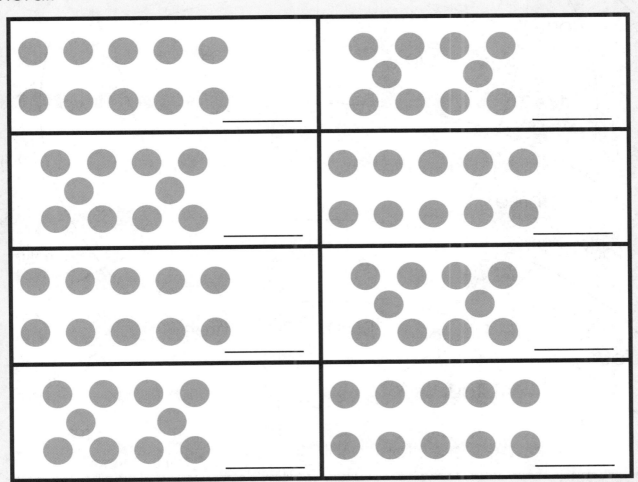

Try This!

Circle each group of 5 dots with a red crayon.

Taking Flight

Directions: Color to find the hidden picture.

one = purple	two = pink	three = yellow
four = blue	five = green	

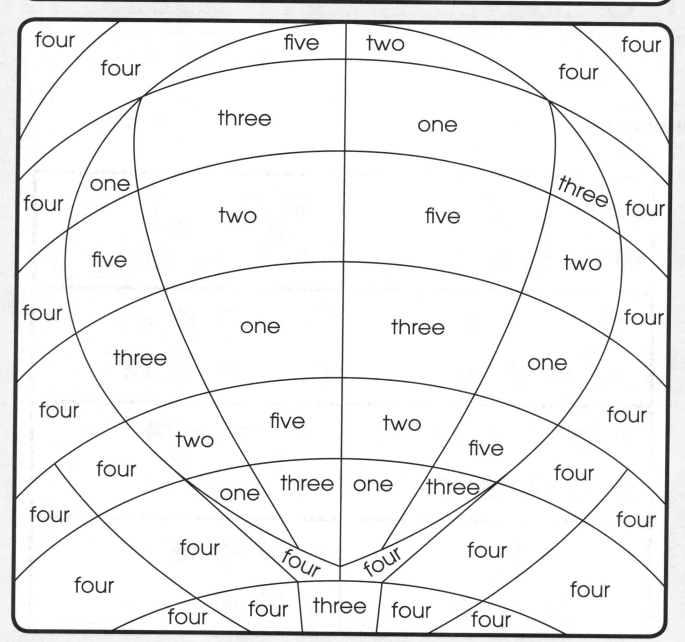

Write the number beside each number word in the picture.

Counting Kernels

Directions: Color to find the hidden picture.

six = orange	seven = blue	eight = green
nine = yellow	ten = brown	

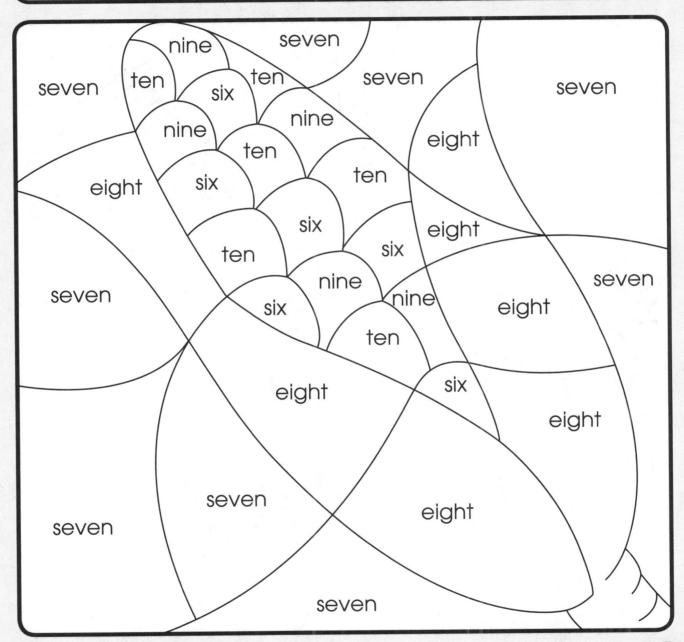

How many different colors were used in the picture?

Pony Piñata

Directions: Count the dots. Color by the code.

3 = red	5 = green
6 = yellow	8 = purple

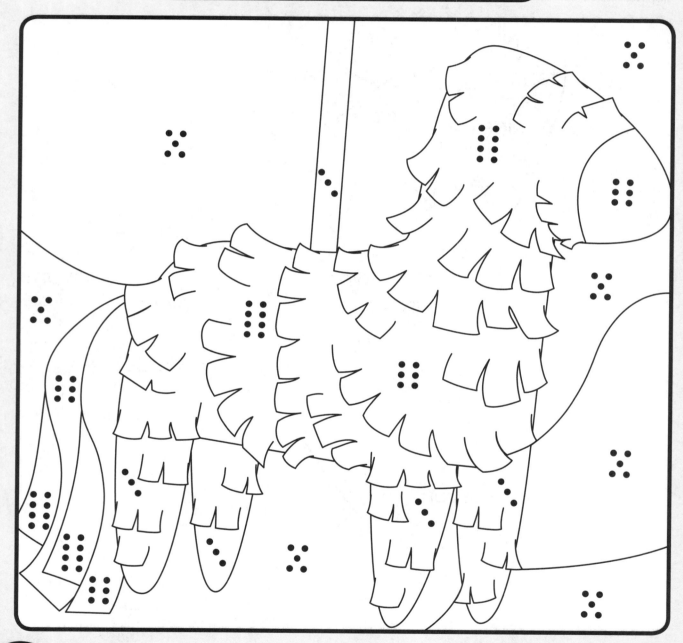

What are piñatas used for?
Write one sentence to tell about piñatas. Ask an adult for help.

Recycled Robot

Directions: Use the code to color the picture.

6 = red   9 = green   7 = blue
10 = yellow   8 = purple

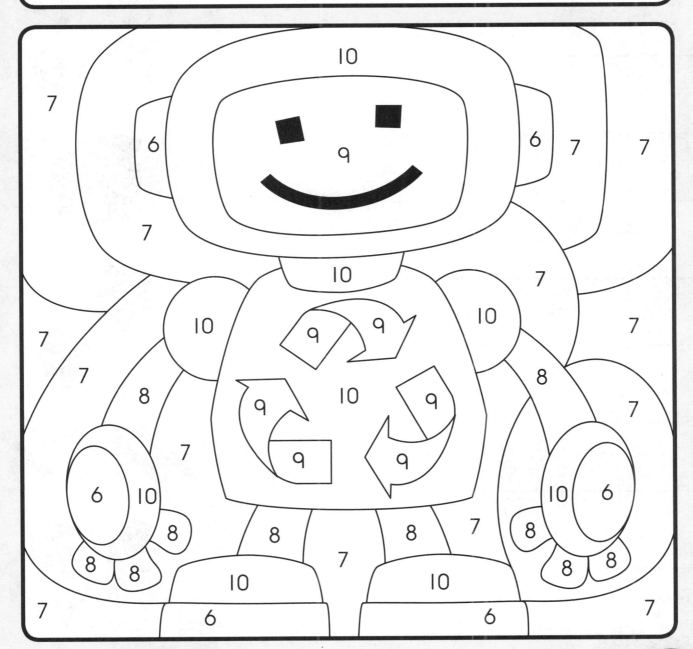

What does the symbol in the middle of the robot mean? Ask an adult for help.

Number Word Match

Directions: Trace the numbers and the words. Draw a line to match the number to the correct picture.

1 one

2 two

3 three

4 four

5 five

Try This!

What is something you would like to have five of? Why?

Count Me In

Directions: Trace the numbers and the words. Draw a line to match the number to the correct picture.

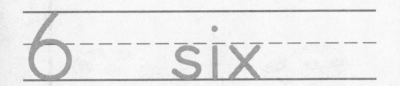

6 six

7 seven

8 eight

9 nine

10 ten

Try This!

Look around your home. Try to find the numbers 6 through 10 around you.

Artist's Palette

Directions: Connect the dots from **0** to **20**. Start at **0**. Color the picture.

Circle all of the odd numbers in the dot-to-dot.

Fill It In

Directions: Write the missing numbers.

1			4		6
		9		11	
	14				18
19				23	
			28		

Color the even numbers red and the odd numbers green.

Numbers to Hop By

Directions: Connect the dots from **0** to **30**. Start at **0**. Color the picture.

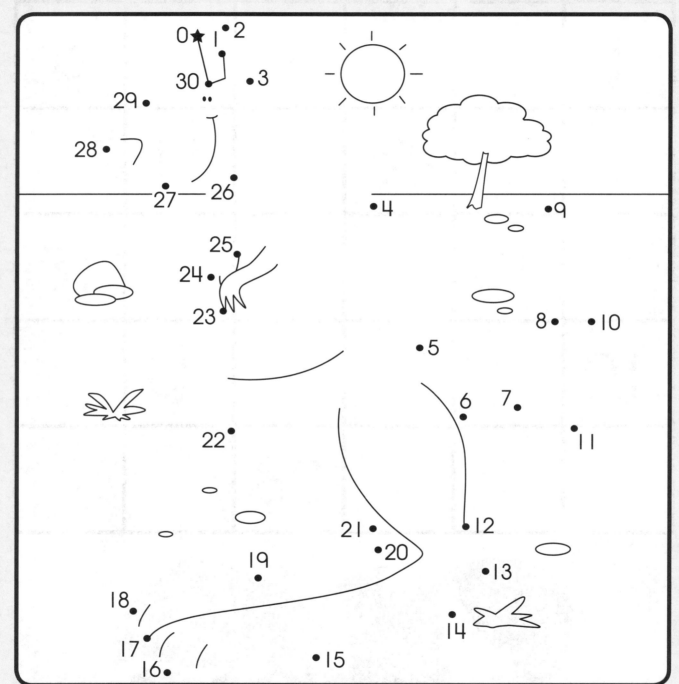

 **Try This!**

What is a kangaroo's baby called? Ask an adult for help.

How Many? Numbers 1–9

Directions: Count the objects in each box. Cut and glue the correct number in each box.

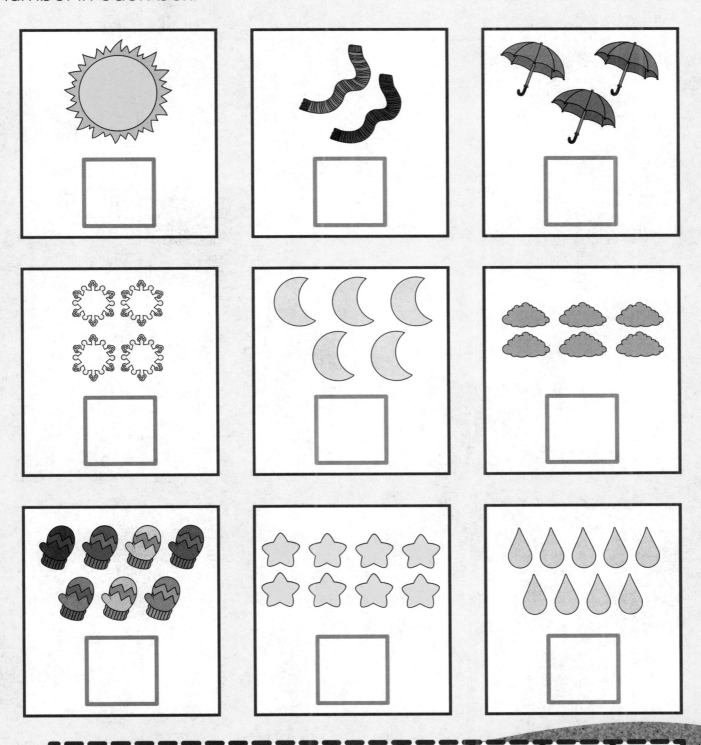

Number Fun

Directions: Count. Write the number. Circle 10 objects in each set.

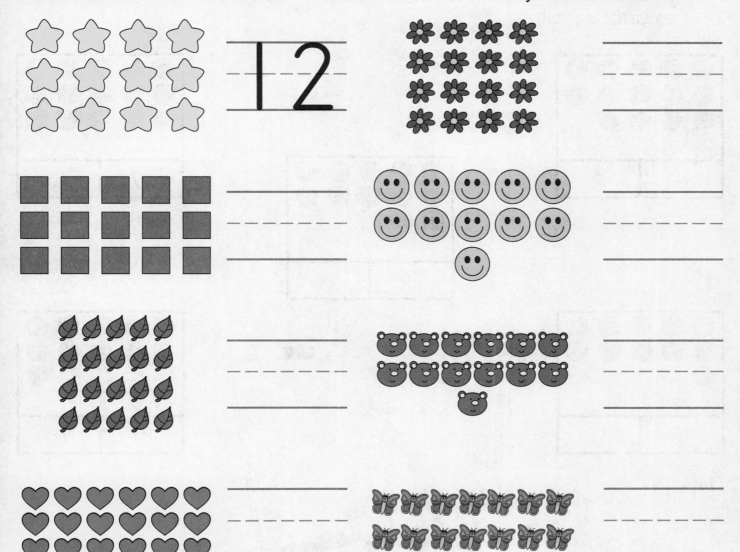

12

Circle the set with the fewest objects.

Directions: Count the dots. Circle the correct number. Draw 20 dots on the artist's picture.

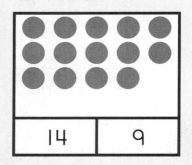

| 14 | 9 |

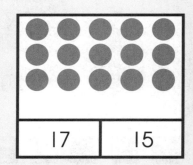

| 17 | 15 |

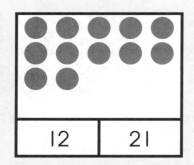

| 12 | 21 |

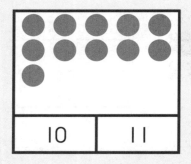

| 10 | 11 |

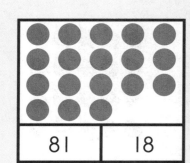

| 81 | 18 |

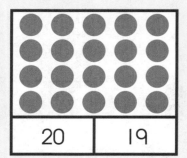

| 20 | 19 |

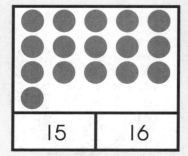

| 15 | 16 |

 **Try This!**

Glue 20 objects on the dots you drew on the artist's picture. Use beans, buttons, or any other craft material.

Yummy Numbers

Directions: Count each set. Cut out the numbers. Glue the correct number in each box.

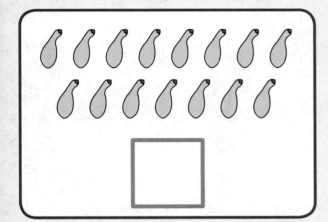

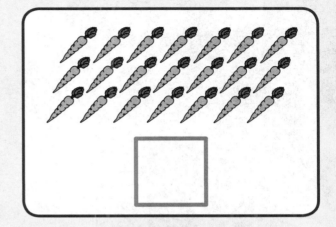

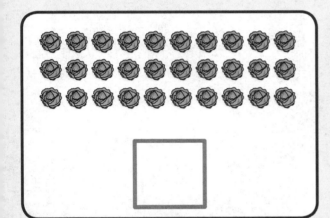

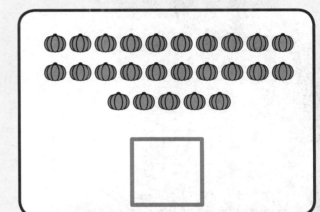

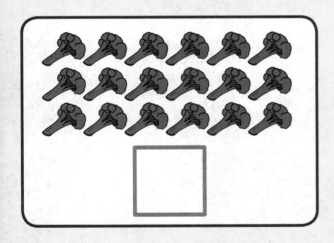

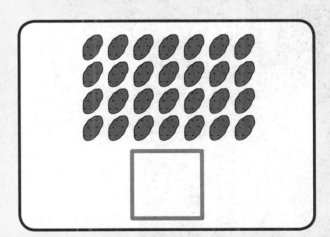

cut

| 15 | 18 | 21 | 25 | 28 | 30 |

Super Numbers and Sets

Directions: Draw a line from each number to the word. Draw the correct number of objects in the box next to the number word.

6   ten

4   three

10   six

3   four

7   nine

9   one

2   seven

8   two

1   five

5   eight

Trace each number word above with a different color of crayon.

Pretty Pumpkin

Directions: Color by the code. Finish coloring the pumpkin.

◯ = red   ▢ = blue   △ = purple

◖ = green   ◇ = yellow   ▭ = pink

 **Try This!**

How many shapes do you see altogether? Write the number.

Color That Shape!

Directions: Follow the directions in each row.

1. Color the circle red.	○ ▭ ▢ △
2. Color the square blue.	○ △ ▢ ▭ ⬭
3. Color the triangle green.	⬭ △ ▢ ○
4. Color the rectangle orange.	▭ ○ ⬭ ⬡
5. Color the rhombus purple.	○ ◇ ▭ △ ▢
6. Color the oval pink.	⬭ ▢ △ ▭

Use the shapes on this page to draw a picture of a robot.
How many shapes can you use?

Shapes in Space

Directions: Find the circles, triangles, squares, ovals, rectangles, and parallelograms. Color them.

Count the shapes. Write the number at the bottom.

Puppy's Picks

Directions: Cut. Glue each object to match its shape. Count. Write the number of sides and corners.

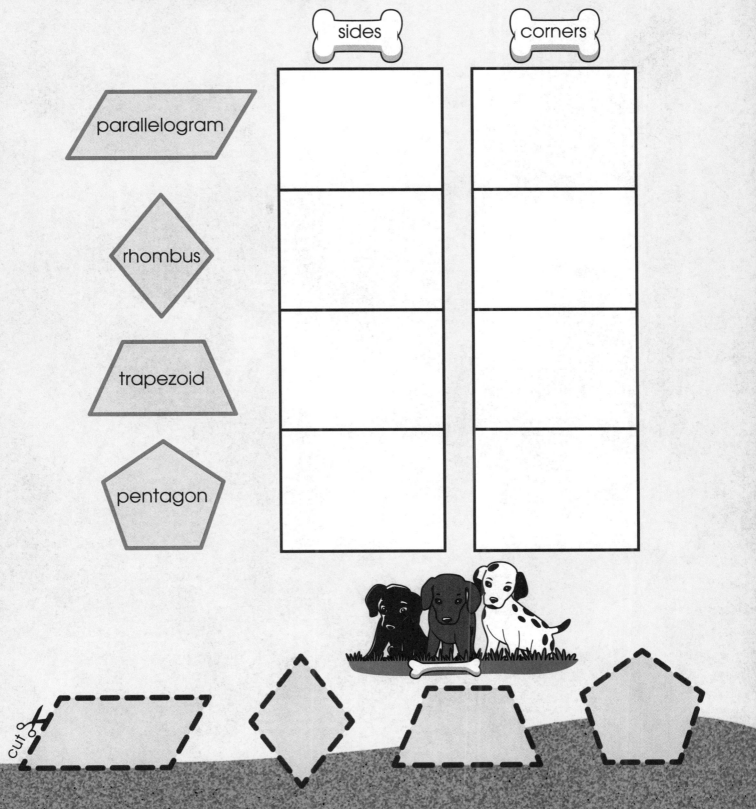

sides

corners

parallelogram

rhombus

trapezoid

pentagon

cut

Drawing Symmetry

Directions: Look at each picture. Draw the other side to match. Trace the lines of symmetry with a crayon.

Find an object with symmetry to trace on a sheet of paper.
Draw a line of symmetry through your drawing.

Starry Symmetry

Directions: Look at each picture. Draw the other side to match. Draw a line of symmetry on the star.

Try This!

Draw half of a shape. Ask a friend to draw the other side of your drawing. Make sure your shape has symmetry.

124

Nature Patterns

Directions: Cut. Glue to finish each pattern.

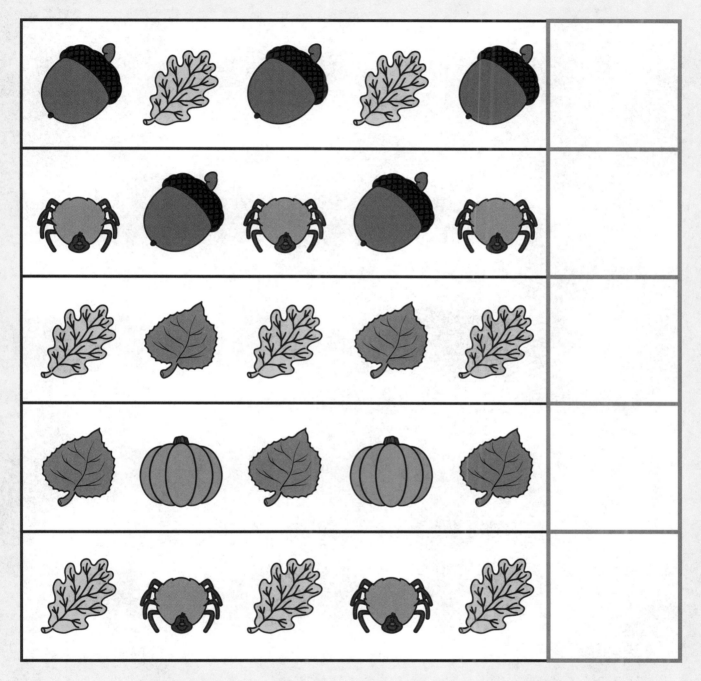

Big Butterflies

Directions: Count. Color the side with more.

On the side with fewer dots, draw enough dots to make the sides equal.

127

Super Sports Sets

Directions: Count. Color the side with less.

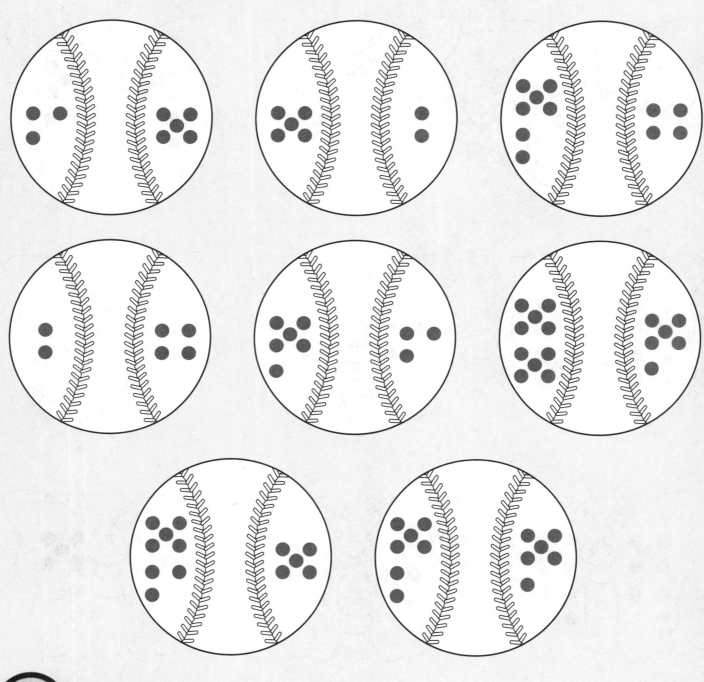

On the side with less, draw enough objects to make the sides equal.

Bunches of Bananas

Directions: Count the bananas in each set. Cut. Glue a monkey under the set of bananas that is greater in each box.

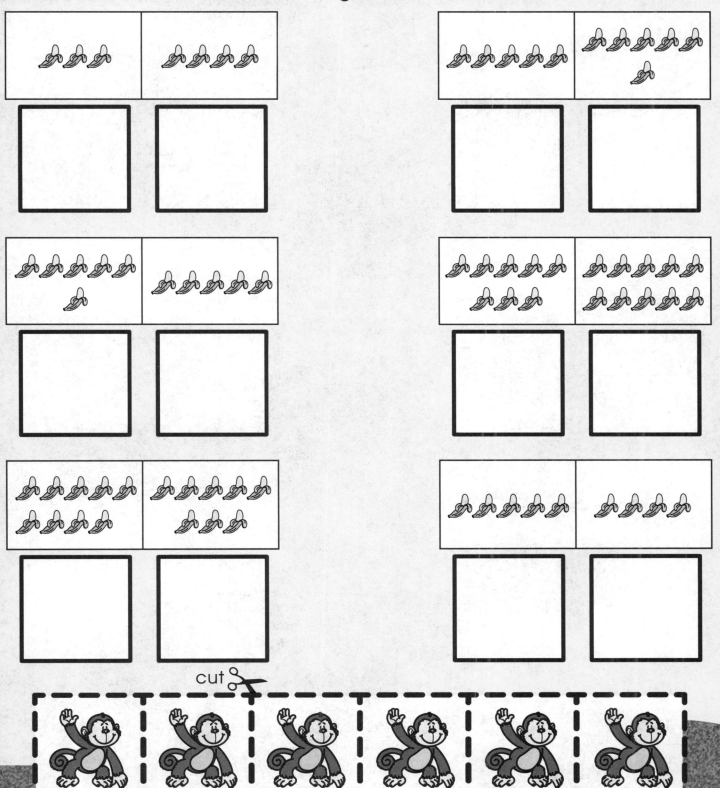

cut ✂

129

Buried Bones

Directions: Count the bones in each set. Cut. Glue a dog under the set of bones that is less in each box.

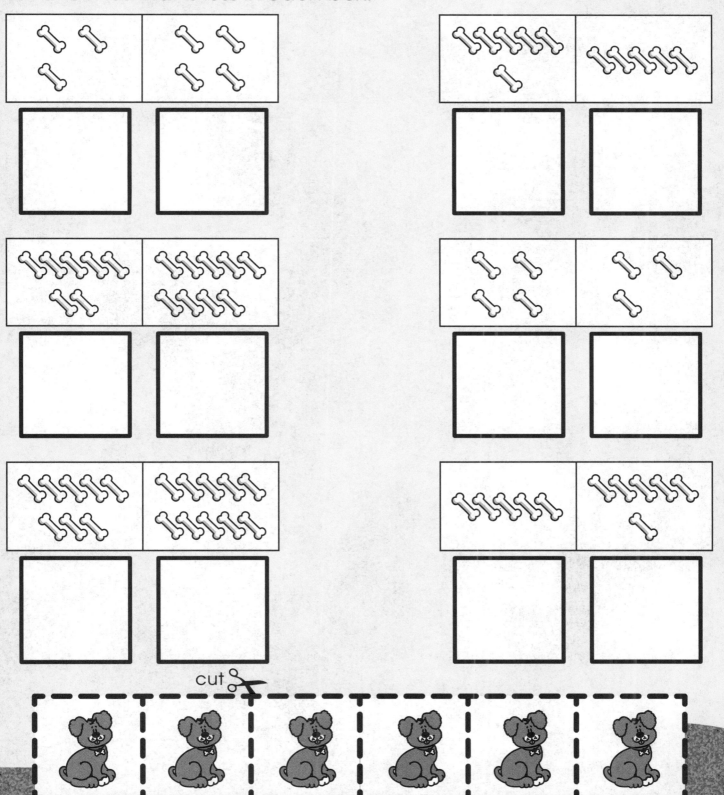

cut

A Bushel of Apples

Directions: Count each set. Draw more apples to make sets of 10.

Put a button, a bean, or other type of counter on each apple as you count.

Shout It Out

Directions: Write each set of numbers from smallest to largest.

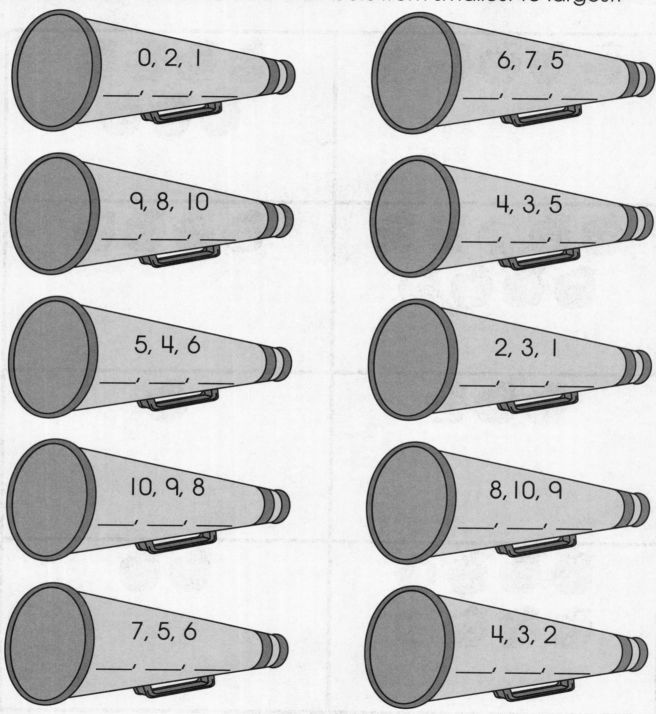

0, 2, 1

___, ___, ___

6, 7, 5

___, ___, ___

9, 8, 10

___, ___, ___

4, 3, 5

___, ___, ___

5, 4, 6

___, ___, ___

2, 3, 1

___, ___, ___

10, 9, 8

___, ___, ___

8, 10, 9

___, ___, ___

7, 5, 6

___, ___, ___

4, 3, 2

___, ___, ___

Try This!

Choose three sets of numbers. Add the numbers of each set together. Write the sums.

First, Second, Third

Directions: Use the code to color the first, second, and third one in each row.

| 1st = green | 2nd = yellow | 3rd = red |

Draw and label a fourth animal in each row.

Monkey Maze

Directions: Color the numbers in order from **10** to **100** to help the monkey find the bananas.

Try This!

Draw three living things on another sheet of paper.

"Hoppy" Counting

Directions: Count by **10**s. Write the missing numbers.

   10, 20, _____ , 40, _____ , 60

   30, _____ , _____ , 60, _____ , 80

   50, _____ , 70 , _____ , _____ , _____

   _____ , 40, 50, _____ , _____ , 80

   _____ , 50, _____ , _____ , 80, _____

Try This!

Circle the largest number in the activity above.

The Ants Go Marching

Directions: Count by **5**s. Color the boxes to show the way to the picnic basket.

Start

☆ 5	10	15	20	25	12
🐜	13	🐜🐜🐜		30	🐜
48	64	45	40	35	86
24	🐜	50	🐜🐜🐜		99
18	🐜	55	60	65	70
37	61	39	🐜	80	75
🐜	96	95	90	85	76
40	23	100			

Finish

"Berry" Good Counting

Directions: Count by **5**s. Touch each number as you count it. Cut. Glue to fill in the missing numbers.

| 5 | 10 | 15 | 20 | 25 | 30 | 35 | 40 | 45 | 50 |

| 5 | | | | 25 |

| | | | | 50 |

| 20 | 30 | 15 | 40 | 35 | 45 | 10 | ✂ cut |

Two by Two

Directions: Cut. Count by **2**s. Glue the numbers in order.

2	4			10
		16		
	24		28	

| 30 | 22 | 8 |

| 14 | 6 | 20 | 12 | 18 | 26 |

cut ✄

Animal Addition

Directions: Count each set of animals. Write the number under each set. Cut and glue the sum at the end of each number sentence.

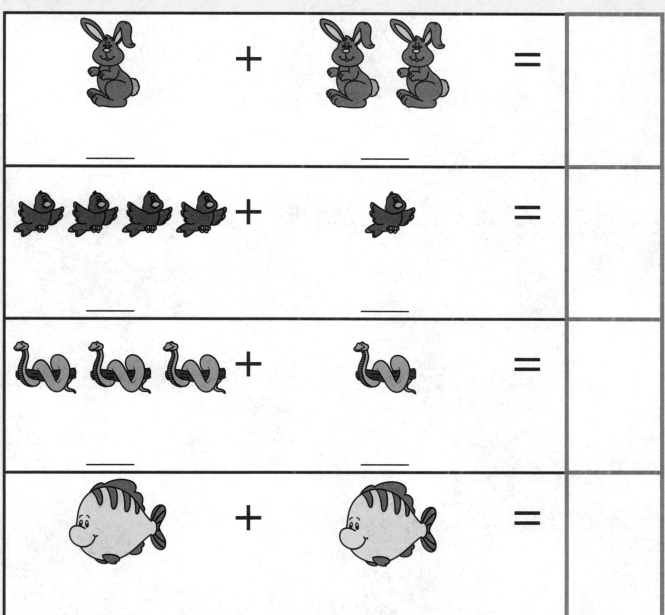

Starry Sums

Directions: Add the two numbers. Write the sum. Color by the code.

3 = green	4 = purple	5 = blue

3 + 1 =

3 + 0 =

2 + 3 =

5 + 0 =

4 + 0 =

4 + 1 =

1 + 2 =

2 + 2 =

2 + 1 =

3 + 2 =

Undersea Adding

Directions: Add each set of numbers. Use the code to color the picture.

3 = blue	2 = pink	4 = yellow	8 = brown
5 = green	6 = orange	7 = purple	

5 + 2 =

1 + 1 =

0 + 3 =

3 + 1 =

3 + 3 =

3 + 0 =

1 + 3 =

4 + 4 =

2 + 3 =

3 + 4 =

5 + 3 =

2 + 6 =

4 + 2 =

2 + 0 =

 **Try This!**

Draw another undersea animal in the picture. Write an addition problem in the animal. Color it by the code.

Domino Addition

Directions: Count the dots on each domino. Solve each problem.

1 + 1 = _____

2 + 1 = _____

2 + 3 = _____

3 + 2 = _____

1 + 3 = _____

3 + 1 = _____

Try This!

Draw your own domino addition problem. Ask a friend to solve your problem.

Dotty Dominoes

Directions: Count the dots on each domino. Solve the problem.

$$\begin{array}{r} 4 \\ +\,6 \\ \hline \end{array}$$

$$\begin{array}{r} 3 \\ +\,4 \\ \hline \end{array}$$

$$\begin{array}{r} 5 \\ +\,0 \\ \hline \end{array}$$

$$\begin{array}{r} 6 \\ +\,1 \\ \hline \end{array}$$

$$\begin{array}{r} 7 \\ +\,3 \\ \hline \end{array}$$

$$\begin{array}{r} 8 \\ +\,2 \\ \hline \end{array}$$

$$\begin{array}{r} 4 \\ +\,5 \\ \hline \end{array}$$

$$\begin{array}{r} 6 \\ +\,3 \\ \hline \end{array}$$

Try This!

Glue a craft material to each dot as you count.
Use beans, buttons, glitter, or other craft materials.

Bouncing, Rolling Fun

Directions: Follow the directions for each row. Write a number sentence to match.

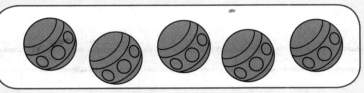 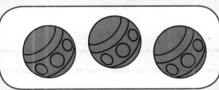

Color 5 green.
Color 3 red.

$\underline{\quad 5 \quad} + \underline{\quad 3 \quad} = \underline{\quad 8 \quad}$

Color 4 yellow.
Color 3 orange.

$\underline{\qquad} + \underline{\qquad} = \underline{\qquad}$

Color 5 blue.
Color 4 yellow.

$\underline{\qquad} + \underline{\qquad} = \underline{\qquad}$

Color 4 red.
Color 6 yellow.

$\underline{\qquad} + \underline{\qquad} = \underline{\qquad}$

Color 4 blue.
Color 2 green.

$\underline{\qquad} + \underline{\qquad} = \underline{\qquad}$

Try This!

Write the sums in order from least to greatest.

Spring Garden

Directions: Add. Use the code to color by number.

10 = green	9 = yellow	8 = brown
7 = orange	6 = blue	5 = gray

- 4 + 5 =
- 3 + 4 =
- 6 + 4 =
- 2 + 8 =
- 5 + 1 =
- 5 + 0 =
- 5 + 4 =
- 9 + 0 =
- 2 + 4 =
- 6 + 1 =
- 6 + 3 =
- 5 + 1 =
- 2 + 3 =
- 1 + 4 =
- 4 + 4 =
- 2 + 6 =
- 4 + 1 =
- 3 + 2 =

Count how many problems were colored for each color.
Write the number in tally marks beside each color in the code.

150

Bye-Bye, Birdie

Directions: Look at the pictures. Write a number sentence that matches the picture. Circle the number of the difference for each problem.

__7__ - __3__ = __4__

7   6   (4)

____ - ____ = ____

7   8   9

____ - ____ = ____

9   10   5

____ - ____ = ____

6   5   4

____ - ____ = ____

6   3   2

____ - ____ = ____

3   5   8

Try This!

Choose three problems in the activity above.
Write an addition sentence that is the opposite of the picture. For example, 4 + 3 = 7.

Disappearing Animals

Directions: Look at the pictures. Write a number sentence that matches the picture. Circle the number of the difference for each problem.

_____ - _____ = _____

3   2   1

_____ - _____ = _____

5   4   3

_____ - _____ = _____

5   6   4

_____ - _____ = _____

0   2   1

_____ - _____ = _____

4   5   6

_____ - _____ = _____

3   2   1

 **Try This!**

Place a counter on each picture. Remove the counters on pictures with an X.
Count the number of counters that are left.

Buttons

Directions: Follow the directions. Write a number sentence for each picture.

Cross out 2. How many are left? 3

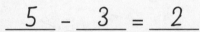

$$\underline{\quad 5 \quad} - \underline{\quad 3 \quad} = \underline{\quad 2 \quad}$$

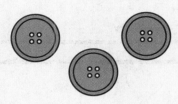

Cross out 1. How many are left?

_____ − _____ = _____

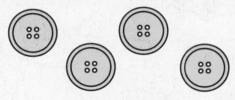

Cross out 3. How many are left?

_____ − _____ = _____

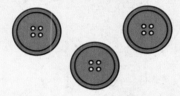

Cross out 0. How many are left?

_____ − _____ = _____

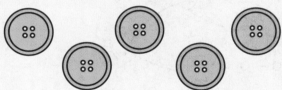

Cross out 4. How many are left?

_____ − _____ = _____

Cross out 2. How many are left?

_____ − _____ = _____

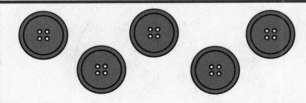

Cross out 3. How many are left?

_____ − _____ = _____

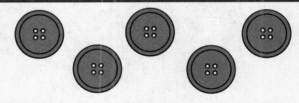

Cross out 5. How many are left?

_____ − _____ = _____

Try This!

Place a real button over each picture. As you follow the directions, remove the buttons. Count the buttons that are left.

Weeding the Garden

Directions: Subtract. Use the code to color by number.

5 = red	2 = blue	3 = green
1 = yellow	0 = brown	4 = orange

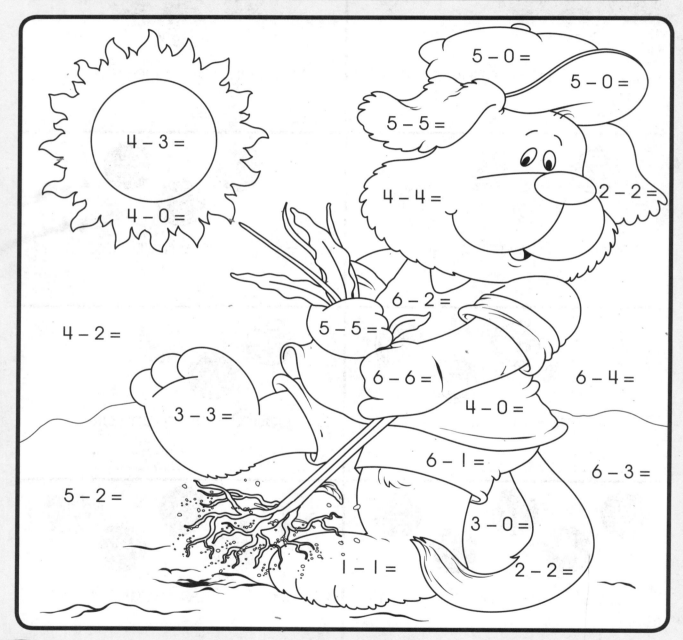

Draw another vegetable in the garden above.
Write a subtraction problem in the vegetable. Color your drawing by the code.

Little Lizards

Directions: Subtract. Use the code to color by number.

1 = yellow	2 = blue	3 = orange	4 = purple

 4 − 1 =

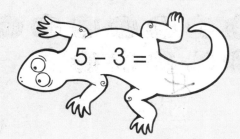 5 − 3 =

 6 − 5 =

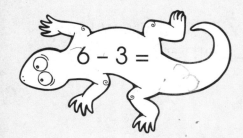 6 − 3 =

 5 − 1 =

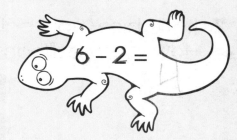 6 − 2 =

 6 − 4 =

5 − 4 =

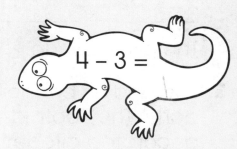 4 − 3 =

 8 − 4 =

7 − 5 =

9 − 6 =

 **Try This!**

Draw three more lizards. Write a subtraction problem in each lizard.
Color the lizards by the code.

Harvest Party

Directions: Read the story problems. Answer the questions. Fill in each blank with the correct answer.

1. Daniel picked 7 pumpkins. Sam picked 5 pumpkins. How many pumpkins did the boys pick altogether?

_____ + _____ = _____

The boys picked _____ pumpkins altogether.

2. Katie blew up 4 balloons for the harvest party. Claire blew up 7. How many balloons did the girls blow up altogether?

_____ + _____ = _____

The girls blew up _____ balloons altogether.

3. Joe and his brother helped their dad decorate tables for the party. They both decorated 6 tables. How many tables were decorated altogether?

_____ + _____ = _____

The boys decorated _____ tables altogether.

Draw a picture of the harvest party.

Rain Forest Walk

Directions: Read the story problems. Answer the questions. Fill in each blank with the correct answer.

1. Three monkeys are resting in a tree. Four alligators are under the tree. How many animals are there in all?

_____ + _____ = _____

_____ animals are in all.

2. Aaron saw 5 colorful frogs on a tree while walking with his parents. Abigail saw 2 more frogs than Aaron. How many frogs did they see in all?

_____ + _____ = _____

Aaron and Abigail saw _____ frogs in all.

3. A leopard was lying in a tree. He saw three monkeys swinging from tree to tree. How many animals were in the trees?

_____ + _____ = _____

A total of _____ animals are in the trees.

Try This!

Draw a picture of one of the animals in the problems above.

Directions: Read the story problems. Answer the questions. Fill in each blank with the correct answer.

1. Parker hit 7 baseballs. Two of them were home runs and went out of the park. How many baseballs were hit in the park?

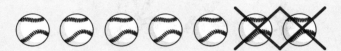

_____ – _____ = _____

He hit _____ baseballs in the park.

2. Eight players are on one team. Four of them are in the dugout. The rest are on the field. How many players are on the field?

_____ – _____ = _____

_____ are on the field.

3. Molly's team had 7 baseball gloves. They shared 3 of those with the other team. How many baseball gloves does Molly's team have left?

_____ – _____ = _____

Molly's team has _____ baseball gloves left.

Write your own baseball story problem. Draw a picture to go with your problem. Ask a friend to solve your story problem.

Shopping for Pets

Directions: Read the story problems. Answer the questions. Fill in each blank with the correct answer.

1. Nine fish were in the tank at the pet store. Bailey bought 5 of the fish. She took them home with her. How many fish are left at the pet store?

_____ – _____ = _____

_____ fish are still in the tank at the pet store.

2. Nine birds were sitting on the perch. Seven jumped down to eat some bird food. How many birds were left on the perch?

_____ – _____ = _____

_____ birds are left on the perch.

3. Kelsey has 10 kittens at the pet shop. She gave 7 kittens away to her friends. How many kittens does she have left?

_____ – _____ = _____

Kelsey has _____ kittens left.

Choose one problem above.
Rewrite the story problem and drawing to make it an addition problem.

Time for School

Directions: Read each story problem. Draw a picture. Answer the question. Fill in the blank with the correct answer.

1. Kayla had 6 pencils. Casey had 2 fewer pencils than Kayla. How many pencils did Casey have?

_____ – _____ = _____

Casey had _____ pencils.

2. Ricky liked to eat grapes at snack time. He had a bag of 12 grapes. He shared half of his grapes with Tammy. How many grapes did each person get?

_____ – _____ = _____

Tammy and Ricky each got _____ grapes.

3. The school had 5 flags outside the building. Two flags had to be taken down every afternoon. How many flags did **not** have to be taken down every day?

_____ – _____ = _____

_____ flags did **not** have to be taken down.

4. Ten children were on the playground. Four of the children could not swing on their own. How many children could swing on their own?

_____ – _____ = _____

_____ children **could** swing on their own.

Try This!

Choose one of the story problems above. Draw a picture to show the story.

Chef's Choice

Directions: Cut. Glue in order.

Menu	
Sunday	pizza
	rice
	taco
	spaghetti
	soup
	chicken
	fish

cut ✂

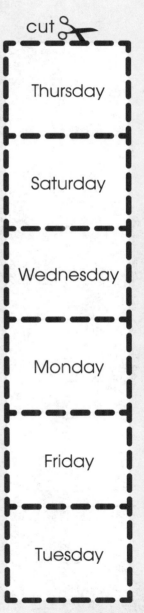

- Thursday
- Saturday
- Wednesday
- Monday
- Friday
- Tuesday

Try This!

What is your favorite meal to eat for dinner? Draw a picture of it.

Monthly Memories

Directions: Cut. Glue the missing months of the year and the pictures in order.

January		March	April
	June		August
September			December

November

July   October   February   May

cut

School Days

Directions: Draw a red rectangle around the name of the month.
Color the names of the days of the week purple.
Color all of the weekend days blue.
Color the 1st Thursday of the month orange.
Color the 4th Monday yellow.
Draw a circle on the last day of the month.

May

Sunday	Monday	Tuesday	Wednesday	Thursday	Friday	Saturday
		1	2	3	4	5
6	7	8	9	10	11	12
13	14	15	16	17	18	19
20	21	22	23	24	25	26
27	28	29	30	31		

What day of the week was the party on? _____

What was the date of the flag ceremony?_____

What day of the week did the class visit the library? _____

What season is this month?

165

What to Wear?

Directions: Look at the calendar. Answer the questions.

April

Sunday	Monday	Tuesday	Wednesday	Thursday	Friday	Saturday
			1 ❄	2	3	4 💧
5	6	7 💧	8	9 ☀	10 ☁	11
12 ☁	13	14 ☀	15	16 💧	17	18 ❄
19	20	21	22 ☁	23	24 ☀	25
26	27 💧	28	29 ☀	30		

Write how many: days _____   days_____

 days_____   days_____

How many days will you need an ? _____

How many days will you need ? _____

 **Try This!**

What type of shoes would you wear on the 7th? Write a sentence to tell your answer.

Find the Right Size

Directions: Circle the largest object in each group.

1.

2.

Directions: Circle the smallest object in each group.

3.
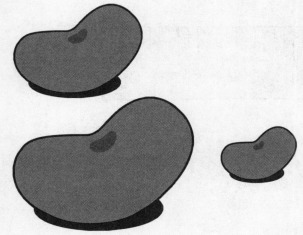

4.

Try This!

Find three books in your library. Order the books from smallest to largest.

Rulers Rule!

Directions: Look at each ruler. Write the length of each object.

1. _____ inches

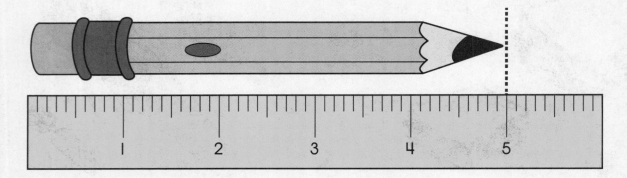

2. _____ inches

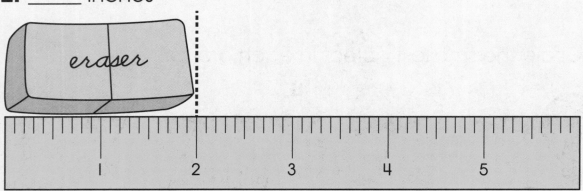

3. _____ inches

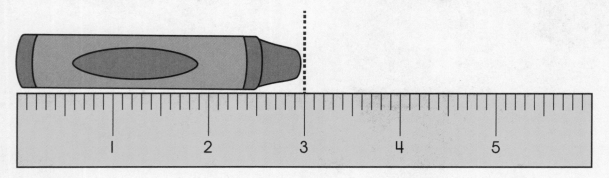

Use a ruler to measure three more objects in your desk or pencil box.

Lining Up

Directions: Use a ruler to measure the length of each line to the nearest inch.

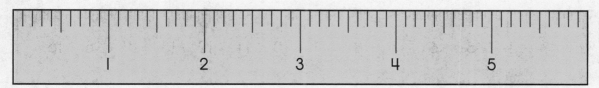

I. _____ _____ inches

2. _____ _____ inches

3. _____ _____ inches

4. _____ _____ inches

5. _____ _____ inch

Glue a piece of yarn along each line.

Count Your Centimeters

Directions: Use a ruler to measure the length of each line to the nearest centimeter.

1. _____ _____ centimeters

2. _____ _____ centimeters

3. _____ _____ centimeters

4. _____ _____ centimeters

5. ____ _____ centimeters

With an adult, go on a measurement walk. Take a centimeter ruler. Measure objects along your walk.

The Hands of Time

Directions: Cut. Glue the numbers to the clock. Add hands with a brass paper fastener.

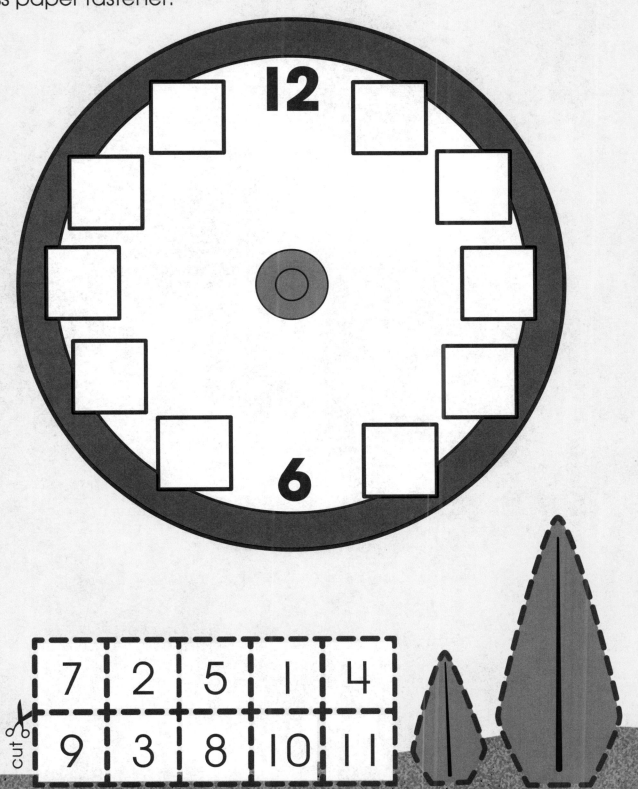

7	2	5	1	4
9	3	8	10	11

cut

Squirrelly Time

Directions: Write the correct time.

Try This!

How many hours passed between the first clock and the second clock in the activity above?

173

Clock Matchup

Directions: Draw a line from each clock to the clock with the matching time.

 **Try This!**

Draw a clock that shows two o'clock.

Time to Match!

Directions: Cut. Glue to show the correct time.

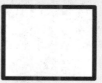

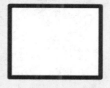

12:00	3:00	8:00	2:00	10:00
6:00	9:00	4:00	7:00	

cut

Make a Graph

Directions: Ask eight friends, "Which of these do you like to play on the most—the swings, the slide, or the seesaw?" Color a box for each answer.

Playground Favorites

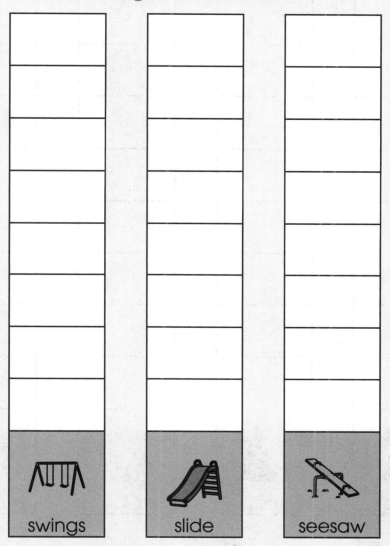

How many? 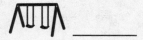 _____  _____  _____

Which was most? _____ Which was least? _____

Which one do you like to play on the most?
Write one complete sentence to tell your answer.

Pet Patrol

Directions: Ask eight friends, "Which pet do you like the best—a dog, a cat, a rabbit, or a hamster?" Color a box for each answer.

Favorite Pets

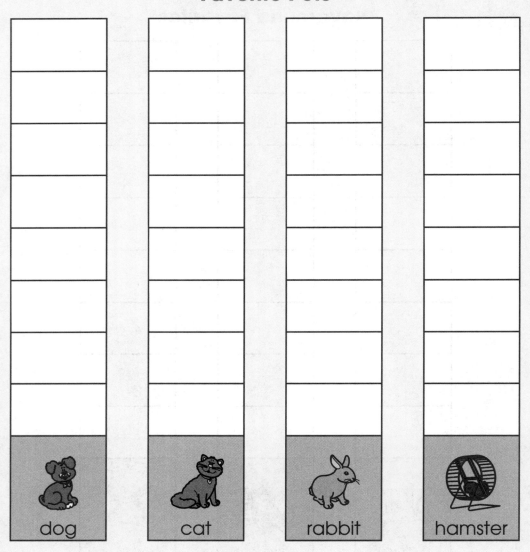

How many? _____ _____ rabbit _____  _____

Which was most? _____ Which was least? _____

Answer Key

Page 11

Butterfly: fish, dog; mitten: snowman, scarf; bus: plane, train; knife: spoon, fork.

Page 13

Row 1: bed; Row 2: owl; Row 3: mitten; Row 4: apple; Row 5: B.

Page 14

blue: X, P, F, T, H, W, A, D, I, Z, S, Z, G, C, X; green: 7, 6, 7, 5, 4, 8, 2, 10, 3, 2, 9.

Page 15

3 letters: six, ten, red, two; 4 letters: five, blue, four, draw; 5 letters: black, seven, color, green.

Page 18

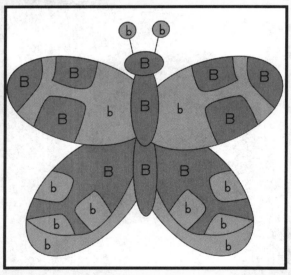

Page 20

Page 22

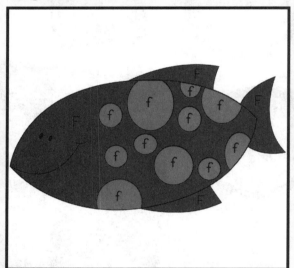

Page 24

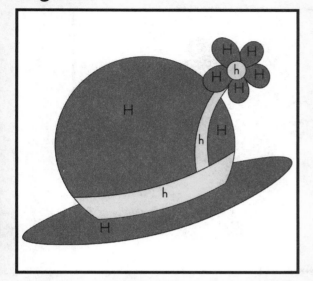

Page 28

Page 26

Page 30

Page 32

Page 36

Page 34

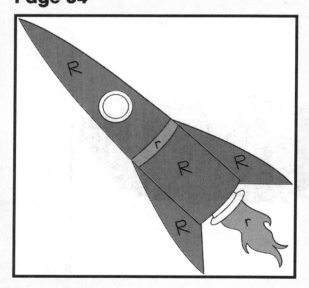

Page 38

Answer Key

Page 40

Page 42

Page 43
Uppercase: R, Q, Y; lowercase: k, e, h, g, t, i.

Page 45
Pairs: D d; M m; F f; N n; J j; G g; C c; B b; A a; E e; H h.

Page 46
Row 1: W w, T t, F f; Row 2: Y y, G g, Q q; Row 3: B b, D d, R r; Row 4: Z z.

Page 47
Row 1: c, h, j; Row 2: d, i, b; Row 3: f, g, e; Row 4: a.

Page 48
Row 1: k, l, n; Row 2: q, o, m; Row 3: p, r, s.

Page 49
Tracks should be glued in alphabetical order.

Page 51

Page 52
green: barn, backpack, bear, bike, bed, bib, bell, box, bird, bone, bee; yellow: dice, desk, dog; blue: cow, corn, cake, can, cup; red: football, feather, fence, feet, fan, fish.

Page 53
Row I: Color goat, gate, guitar. G g;
Row 2: Color hat, horse, hand. H h; Row
3: Color jug, jet, jar. J j; Row 4: Color king,
key, kangaroo. K k.

Page 55
Row I: web, bed, leg; Row 2: jet, dog,
vest; Row 3: tent, net, pot.

Page 56
yellow: lion, lemon, lamp, leaf, leg, lock,
lips, ladder; brown: nail, nurse, needle,
net; purple: mop, map, mitten, mug,
moon, mat, milk, mouse, mask, magnet;
blue: pear, pin, penny, pencil, pot,
penguin, pea, pie, peach, pan.

Page 57
Rr: rabbit, rainbow, rug; Ss: six, sun, sock;
Tt: table, tent, turtle; Vv: violin, valentine.

Page 59
Row I: top, barn, net; Row 2: drum, saw,
goat; Row 3: cab, roof, book.

Page 60
Row I: barn (blue), bread (orange),
jeep (green); Row 2: lamp (green), sled
(orange), spoon (blue).

Page 61
Column I: hand, flag, web; Column 2:
can, mop, wheel.

Page 63
cl: clock, cloud; pl: plant, plane; st:
stamp, star.

Page 65
dr: drum, dress; sk: skate, skunk; sn: snail,
snake.

Page 67
gr: grapes, grill; dr: drum, drill; st: stapler,
star.

Page 69
Row I: thumb (yellow), shoe (blue),
chips (red); Row 2: whale (green), chair
(red), thimble (yellow); Row 3: wheel
(green), shirt (blue), whisker (green).

Page 70
Row I: one, two, two; Row 2: one, two,
one; Row 3: three, three, three; Row 4:
one, two, one.

Page 71
Row I: goat (blue), shirt (blue), flower
(yellow), bug (blue); Row 2: pumpkin
(yellow), moon (blue), butterfly (orange),
dog (blue); Row 3: ice cream (yellow),
bird (blue), banana (orange), rug (blue);
Row 4: cat (blue), leaf (blue), castle
(yellow), sandwich (yellow); Row 5:
ladybug (orange), kangaroo (orange),
giraffe (yellow), tomato (orange); Row 6:
clown (blue), star (blue), ship (blue), bee
(blue).

Page 72
Row 1: stamp; Row 2: corn; Row 3: vest; Row 4: drill; Row 5: jet.

Page 73
Row 1: chair/pear, log/dog; Row 2: boat/coat, plane/train; Row 3: log/frog, mop/hop; Row 4: bat/hat, man/can.

Page 74
Balloons should be colored as they are labeled.

Page 75
Gum balls should be colored as they are labeled.

Page 76

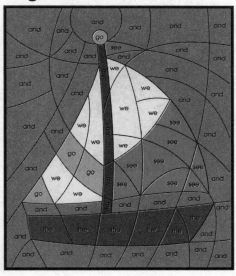

Page 77

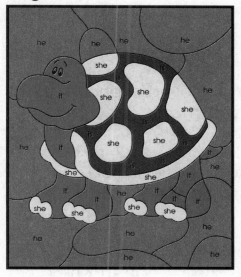

Page 78
Bag, hat, cat, bat, fan, lamp, cap, mask.

Page 79
Pen, net, bed, bell, tent, web, ten, dress.

Page 80
Pin, hill, bib, ring, igloo, wig.

Page 81
Lock, top, clock, box, pot, mop, sock.

Page 82
Cup, bus, truck, rug, sun, jug.

Page 83
Short a: chain, mane, rain, gate; Long a: cap, tag, bag, bat.

Page 85
Short e: teeth, feet, seat, pea; Long e: bed, leg, well, neck.

Page 87
Short i: fire, tire, bike, tie; Long i: wig, six, fish, zipper.

Page 89
Short o: boat, globe, nose, phone; Long o: lock, top, dog, mop.

Page 91
Short u: suit, tube, cube, juice; Long u: puddle, nuts, sun, duck.

Page 93
1. wig; 2. cup; 3. nest; 4. bat; 5. log; 6. duck; 7. pin; 8. shell; 9. hat; 10. chick; 11. fan; 12. rug; 13. mop; 14. frog; 15. bed; 16. lock.

Page 94
Row 1: octopus (green), duck (purple); Row 2: fish (yellow), bat (blue); Row 3: apple (blue), umbrella (purple); Row 4: web (red), bell (red).

Page 96
Row 1: 0, 1; Row 2: 1, 1; Row 3: 1, 0; Row 4: 0, 1.

Page 97
Row 1: 3, 3; Row 2: 2, 3; Row 3: 3, 2; Row 4: 2, 2.

Page 98
Row 1: 4, 5; Row 2: 5, 4; Row 3: 5, 4; Row 4: 4, 5.

Page 99
Row 1: 7, 7; Row 2: 6, 6; Row 3: 7, 6; Row 4: 7, 6.

Page 100
Row 1: 8, 9; Row 2: 9, 8; Row 3: 8 ,9; Row 4: 8, 9.

Page 101
Row 1: 10, 10; Row 2: 10, 10; Row 3: 10, 10; Row 4: 10, 10.

Page 102

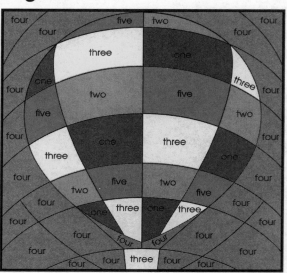

Page 103

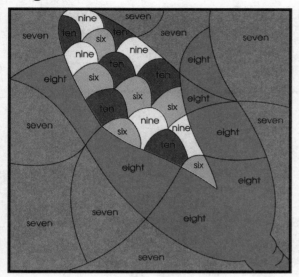

Page 104

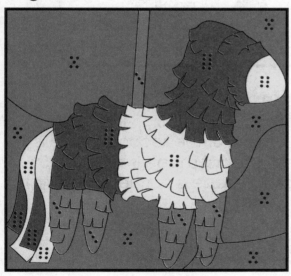

Page 105

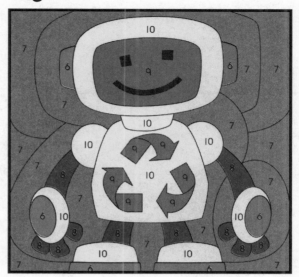

Page 106

One apple; two trees; three fish; four soccer balls; five pencils.

Page 107

Six rockets; seven bears; eight crabs; nine stars; ten flowers.

Page 108

Page 109

2, 3, 5, 7, 8, 10, 12, 13, 15, 16, 17, 20, 21, 22, 24, 25, 26, 27, 29, 30.

Page 110

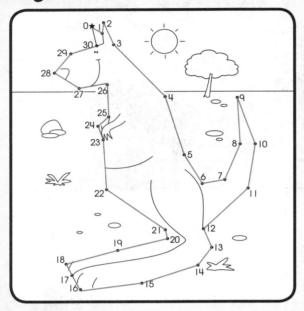

Page 111

Row 1: 1, 2, 3; Row 2: 4, 5, 6; Row 3: 7, 8, 9.

Page 113

Row 1: 16; Row 2: 15, 11; Row 3: 20, 13; Row 4: 18, 14; Row 5: 19, 17.

Page 114

Column 1: 14, 11, 20; Column 2: 12; Column 3: 15, 18, 16.

Page 115

15 eggplants, 21 carrots, 30 lettuces, 25 pumpkins, 18 broccolis, 28 potatoes.

Page 117

6 six; 4 four; 10 ten; 3 three; 7 seven; 9 nine; 2 two; 8 eight; 1 one; 5 five.

Page 118

Page 119

1. The first shape is red.; 2. The third shape is blue.; 3. The second shape is green.; 4. The first shape is orange.; 5. The second shape is purple.; 6. The first shape is pink.

Page 120

Page 121
Parallelogram: 4 sides, 4 corners;
Rhombus: 4 sides, 4 corners; Trapezoid:
4 sides, 4 corners; Pentagon: 5 sides, 5
corners.

Page 123

 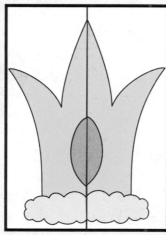

Page 124

Page 125
Row 1: yellow leaf; Row 2: acorn; Row
3: green leaf; Row 4: pumpkin; Row 5:
spider.

Page 127
Row 1: right side, left side, right side; Row
2: right side, left side, left side; Row 3:
right side, right side, right side.

Page 128
Row 1: left side, right side, right side; Row
2: left side, right side, right side; Row 3:
right side, right side.

Page 129
Row 1: right box, right box; Row 2: left
box, right box; Row 3: left box, left box.

Page 131
Row 1: left box, right box; Row 2: left box, right box; Row 3: left box, left box.

Page 133
Row 1: draw 5 apples; draw 3 apples; Row 2: draw 1 apple; draw 6 apples; Row 3: draw 7 apples; draw 9 apples; Row 4: draw 2 apples; draw 8 apples.

Page 134
Row 1: 0, 1, 2; 5, 6, 7; Row 2: 8, 9, 10; 3, 4, 5; Row 3: 4, 5, 6; 1, 2, 3; Row 4: 8, 9, 10; 8, 9, 10; Row 5: 5, 6, 7; 2, 3, 4.

Page 135
Row 1: green, yellow, red; Row 2: green, yellow, red; Row 3: green, yellow, red.

Page 136
Color in order: 10, 20, 30, 40, 50, 60, 70, 80, 90, 100.

Page 137
Row 1: 30, 50; Row 2: 40, 50, 70; Row 3: 60, 80, 90, 100; Row 4: 30, 60, 70; Row 5: 40, 60, 70, 90.

Page 138
Color in order: 5, 10, 15, 20, 25, 30, 35, 40, 45, 50, 55, 60, 65, 70, 75, 80, 85, 90, 95, 100.

Page 139
10, 15, 20, 30, 35, 40, 45.

Page 141
6, 8, 12, 14, 18, 20, 22, 26, 30.

Page 143
Row 1: $1 + 2 = 3$; Row 2: $4 + 1 = 5$; Row 3: $3 + 1 = 4$; Row 4: $1 + 1 = 2$.

Page 145
$3 + 1 = 4$ (purple); $3 + 0 = 3$ (green); $2 + 3 = 5$ (blue); $5 + 0 = 5$ (blue); $4 + 0 = 4$ (purple); $1 + 2 = 3$ (green); $4 + 1 = 5$ (blue); $2 + 2 = 4$ (purple); $3 + 2 = 5$ (blue); $2 + 1 = 3$ (green).

Page 146
blue: $0 + 3 = 3$, $3 + 0 = 3$; pink: $1 + 1 = 2$, $2 + 0 = 2$; yellow: $3 + 1 = 4$, $1 + 3 = 4$; green: $2 + 3 = 5$; orange: $3 + 3 = 6$, $4 + 2 = 6$; purple: $5 + 2 = 7$, $3 + 4 = 7$; brown: $4 + 4 = 8$, $5 + 3 = 8$, $2 + 6 = 8$.

Page 147
$1 + 1 = 2$; $2 + 1 = 3$; $2 + 3 = 5$; $3 + 2 = 5$; $1 + 3 = 4$; $3 + 1 = 4$.

Page 148
$4 + 6 = 10$; $3 + 4 = 7$; $5 + 0 = 5$; $6 + 1 = 7$; $7 + 3 = 10$; $8 + 2 = 10$; $4 + 5 = 9$; $6 + 3 = 9$.

Page 149
4 yellow + 3 orange = 7; 5 blue + 4 yellow = 9; 4 red + 6 yellow = 10; 4 blue + 2 green = 6.

Page 150
green: $6 + 4 = 10$, $2 + 8 = 10$; yellow: $4 + 5 = 9$, $6 + 3 = 9$, $9 + 0 = 9$, $5 + 4 = 9$; brown: $4 + 4 = 8$, $2 + 6 = 8$; orange: $3 + 4 = 7$, $6 + 1 = 7$; blue: $5 + 1 = 6$, $2 + 4 = 6$, $5 + 1 = 6$; gray: $5 + 0 = 5$, $2 + 3 = 5$, $4 + 1 = 5$, $3 + 2 = 5$, $1 + 4 = 5$.

Page 151

9 – 1 = 8; 10 – 5 = 5; 5 – 1 = 4; 6 – 3 = 3; 8 – 5 = 3.

Page 152

2 – 1 = 1; 4 – 1 = 3; 5 – 1 = 4; 1 – 1 = 0; 6 – 2 = 4; 3 – 1 = 2.

Page 153

3 – 1 = 2; 4 – 3 = 1; 3 – 0 = 3; 5 – 4 = 1; 4 – 2 = 2; 5 – 3 = 2; 5 – 5 = 0.

Page 154

red: 5 – 0 = 5, 5 – 0 = 5, 6 – 1 = 5; blue: 4 – 2 = 2, 6 – 4 = 2; green: 5 – 2 = 3, 3 – 0 = 3, 6 – 3 = 3; yellow: 4 – 3 = 1; brown: 5 – 5 = 0, 2 – 2 = 0, 4 – 4 = 0, 5 – 5 = 0, 6 – 6 = 0, 3 – 3 = 0, 1 – 1 = 0, 2 – 2 = 0; orange: 6 – 2 = 4, 4 – 0 = 4, 4 – 0 = 4.

Page 155

4 – 1 = 3 (orange); 5 – 3 = 2 (blue); 6 – 5 = 1 (yellow); 6 – 3 = 3 (orange); 5 – 1 = 4 (purple); 6 – 2 = 3 (orange); 6 – 4 = 2 (blue); 5 – 4 = 1 (yellow); 4 – 3 = 1 (yellow); 8 – 4 = 4 (purple); 7 – 5 = 2 (blue); 9 – 6 = 3 (orange).

Page 156

1. 7 + 5 = 12, 12 pumpkins; 2. 7 + 4 = 11, 11 balloons; 3. 6 + 6 = 12, 12 tables.

Page 157

1. 3 + 4 = 7, 7 animals; 2. 5 + 7 = 12, 12 frogs; 3. 1 + 3 = 4, 4 animals.

Page 158

1. 7 – 2 = 5, 5 baseballs; 2. 8 – 4 = 4, 4 players; 3. 7 – 3 = 4, 4 gloves.

Page 159

1. 9 – 5 = 4, 4 fish; 2. 9 – 7 = 2, 2 birds; 3. 10 – 7 = 3, 3 kittens.

Page 160

1. 6 – 2 = 4, 4 pencils; 2. 12 – 6 = 6, 6 grapes; 3. 5 – 2 = 3, 3 flags; 4. 10 – 4 = 6, 6 children.

Page 161

Monday, Tuesday, Wednesday, Thursday, Friday, Saturday.

Page 163

February, May, July, October, November.

Page 165

May

Sunday	Monday	Tuesday	Wednesday	Thursday	Friday	Saturday
		1	2	3	4	5
6	7	8	9	10	11	12
13	14	15	16	17	18	19
20	21	22	23	24	25	26
27	28	29	30	31		

Monday; Friday; Wednesday.

Page 166

2; 4; 3; 4; 4; 4.

Page 167

1.

2.

3.

4.

Page 168
1. 5; 2. 2; 3. 3.

Page 169
1. 4; 2. 5; 3. 2; 4. 3; 5. 1.

Page 170
1. 7; 2. 5; 3. 9; 4. 11; 5. 2.

Page 171
Clockwise: 1, 2, 3, 4, 5, 7, 8, 9, 10, 11.

Page 173
Row 1: 10:00, 6:00, 11:00, 7:00; Row 2: 12:00, 4:00; Row 3: 5:00, 9:00; Row 4: 3:00, 1:00.

Page 174

Page 175
Row 1: 4:00, 8:00, 3:00; Row 2: 12:00, 9:00, 7:00; Row 3: 2:00, 10:00, 6:00.

Page 177
Answers will vary.

Page 178
Answers will vary.